Praise for

You Don't Look Your Age...
and Other Fairy Tales

————

"This book is gorgeous. I was blown away. The piece about Nevins's mother is stunning. There is such range to this collection. Funny but always honest."
—DELIA EPHRON

"Brave, honest, and inspiring." —EDIE FALCO

"Fearless! Funny! Honest! I loooove it!" —DIANE VON FURSTENBERG

"Funny, sad, insightful, clever, touching! I was immediately captivated. . . . There were moments when I thought Nevins was sharing secrets with me. . . . I loved them all. This was a special read, and when I'd finished I felt I'd been given an unexpected present." —BARBARA TAYLOR BRADFORD

"Super Woman—surely the epic documentary film queen of our times— beautiful, witty, wild, sexy, and insane, tells all (or as much of it as allowed). Join her with your own self-doubt in truth-telling glory. WOW! Dynamite! And why did she do it? The astounding UNIVERSE triumphs with the answer."
—LIZ SMITH

"The glass ceiling–shattering president of HBO Documentary Films turns the lens on herself in an Ephron-esque memoir that probes the petty, the poignant, and the heroic." —O, THE OPRAH MAGAZINE

You Don't Look Your Age . . .

AND OTHER FAIRY TALES

You Don't
Look Your Age . . .
AND OTHER FAIRY TALES

Sheila Nevins

FLATIRON
BOOKS
NEW YORK

A number of stories in this book are products of the author's imagination, and the author has also changed the names and identifying characteristics of certain individuals mentioned in this book to protect their privacy.

www.flatironbooks.com

The Library of Congress has cataloged the hardcover edition as follows:

Names: Nevins, Sheila author.
Title: You don't look your age and other fairy tales / Sheila Nevins.
Description: First edition. | New York : Flatiron Books, 2017.
Identifiers: LCCN 2017003050 | ISBN 9781250111302 (hardcover) |
    ISBN 9781250111326 (ebook)
Subjects: LCSH: Nevins, Sheila. | Women television producers and
    directors—United States—Biography.
Classification: LCC PN1992.4.N35 A3 2017 | DDC 791.4302'32092
    [B]—dc23
LC record available at https://lccn.loc.gov/2017003050

ISBN 978-1-250-11131-9 (trade paperback)

Our books may be purchased in bulk for promotional, educational, or business use. Please contact your local bookseller or the Macmillan Corporate and Premium Sales Department at 1-800-221-7945, extension 5442, or by email at MacmillanSpecialMarkets@macmillan.com.

First Flatiron Books Paperback Edition: April 2019

10 9 8 7 6 5 4 3 2 1

This book is for my son, David Koch, who has appropriately named me Momster. And for my husband, Sidney, who has curbed Momster's destructive self in the kindest way possible.

Contents

You Don't Look Your Age . . .

AND OTHER FAIRY TALES

Why She Wrote
When She Wrote

I'VE SPENT most of my life making documentaries. And I've spent most of this time hiding behind the people in the documentaries. If they were sad or glad, rich or poor, smart or dumb, killers or philanthropists, they would do the talking, they would do the confessing. These were their stories being told, never mine.

What scares me about the alternative? I guess me. I have no trouble speaking my mind in private or asking other people their deepest secrets. I'm not shy and am known to be quite outspoken when it comes to my opinions (especially in an editing room). But I've always kept my personal true confessions close to the vest. I have lived a life inhibited when it comes to self-revelation.

And so, why a change of heart now? Why a book of true and sad and sometimes silly essays? Well, many years ago I was working on a film about the Gray Panthers, a group formed to confront ageism, never thinking I would be a member. Maggie Kuhn, the founder, and I became friends—though generations apart. I once asked Maggie about getting old and fighting back, and she said it was the next great frontier. The great thing about aging, she said, was that at last you could say what you wanted, and do what you wanted, and be who you wanted. All of these years, the subjects in my films have given me their stories. Now it's my turn. I am now at that age where I feel as if I can say what I want; I have no reason to hold back. So, finally, here are my stories.

Is this what it feels like to spill it all out? Well, I'm still not 100 percent front and center. In this book, I'm somewhat undercover—some of the time hiding behind a Priscilla or a Melissa or an Anthea or a Trudie. And sometimes I'm simply me. All me? The truth of what is me is yours to handpick. The "I" is not always me—or is it? Your guess. I'm telling you what I've been told, telling you whom I knew, telling you what I thought, telling you what I do, telling you who I imagine. Maybe I'm hiding a bit, but trust me, I never lie about what I think to be true. You don't have to like the different voices here, but they always tell it like it is or how they believe it was.

The camera is on me now, along with my somewhat imaginary friends, and all my dirty linens are hanging out there. So what if they're polyester?

Facing Face-lifts

1.

"Dr. Baker," I said, "I look awful."

He looked at me with a tragic smile and said, "Fear not. We can do a lift. You'll be just fine."

"I'm fifty-six," I said. "And I think it's about time. Don't you?"

He put his arm around me and said sorrowfully, "It's time."

"Is there anything less invasive than a lift?" I had heard about a nip-and-tucky kind of thing.

"We'll fix you up. Don't worry," he said. "You'll look seven years younger."

"And how long will that me last?" I asked.

"Some seven years," he said.

He gave me a mirror, a hand mirror, under the brightest of fluorescent lights. It said MAGNIFIER X8.

I looked in. I got dizzy and started to gasp. Clearly there was no way out.

In the mirror I saw a wrinkled, witchlike, scrunched up, squashed face.

The mirror spoke to me menacingly, whispering in my ear. It said, *"Without any doubt, you are not the fairest of them all. You are not fair at all!"*

I put the mirror down quickly so Dr. Baker would not hear it.

"How long will it take?" I asked the doctor cavalierly. "This new me?"

"If you do an eye lift, two weeks. Without that, maybe nine days," he said. "In any case, it varies. And you can tell them at work that you're going on a vacation."

"Okay, I'll do both eyes and face," I said. I wanted to get it over with at once.

And the hand mirror said, though indirectly, I had no choice.

2.

I made a date for the new me, three months away.

How would I face myself, I thought, with a new face?

And how awful I really looked! Why hadn't anyone told me?

But then again, not everyone has fluorescent lighting and a x8 magnifying mirror.

Most of my age-appropriate friends said I looked pretty good. But let's face it, they had age-related dimming vision.

———————

I left his office and hailed a taxi. My heart was still racing. Was I brave enough to go through with this superficial scalping?

To make matters worse, the traffic was awful.

I told the driver to slow down, please. He took it personally. He said he hadn't had an accident in twenty years.

I explained, with my regular excuse, that I thought I might be pregnant.

He looked in the rearview mirror, and this is the truth, he said, "You don't look like you could be pregnant."

Okay, Dr. Baker. That was it.

The driver must have been a plant. The cab had been too easy to get. Baker probably owned the cab company.

We laughed a little, the driver and me, and I told him he was right.

I admitted to a bad back and told him I was forty-eight.

Lying about increasing numbers had become part of everyday life.

I remember nostalgically the days when I asked them to slow down because of my pregnancy, and taxi drivers would congratulate me and ask if it was a boy or a girl.

And now I have to lie even more. I have to lie at work about going on vacation.

Lies, lies, lies.

But there was no other choice. It was now or never.

This was the right time to eradicate the old me. I knew it.

I must be perpetually one age—and I picked fifty-one and six months.

This would be where I would stay forever.

———————

You see, I must be young at any price.

Young was in.

I worked in media.

Nobody wanted advice from an old broad.

My bosses wanted a young audience.

Had it occurred to them that an older brain could think smart and young?

I thought most likely not.

In any case, I had to hide my age.

For those who knew the true number, they must be rehearsed to say, "My god, you don't look your age!"

That might give me comfort.

3.

I told my husband and my son about my upcoming operation.

Each extolled my present beauty and assured me of my imminent death by surgery.

"It's ridiculous," my son said. "You'll look like Michael Jackson."

My husband said, "You look fine just the way you are."

"Okay, okay," I said to them both. "I'm beautiful enough. But not young enough. Maybe I'm young enough, but I'm not young enough for the rest of the world."

Then, while waiting for this miracle, my Barnard College fortieth reunion arrived.

I opened the door marked with my graduation year.

Old ladies glared at me through thick glasses. I closed the door quickly.

This must be the wrong room, I thought.

Hadn't they heard of contacts? Old ladies with advanced degrees and high IQs.

Barnard College was a place where brains were supposed to be more important than beauty.

I pretended that was true but never bought into that philosophy.

I opened the door again and walked bravely into the room.

"Oh my God," said an elderly classmate. "You look exactly the same as when we graduated."

"You do too," I said.

This old lady was me as well.

And we were lying to each other.

4.

The day came.

After a sleepless night, my superficial self arrived at Dr. Baker's office at 5 a.m.

In addition to being fearful of the anesthesia and ultimately of my death, I was betraying my liberal, earnest, sixties self.

Could this artificial mannequin be me? Could this still be the Woodstock, March on Washington, antiapartheid liberal? Could I be this deceptive mid-fifties liar? Lying to taxi drivers and trying to keep seven years at bay? What happened to the honor system?

I moved onto the gurney.

I was then prepped by an annoying nurse who gave me enough Valium that I would have allowed the Boston Strangler to do the operation.

I had given my life to vanity.

Here I was—brainless, vain, terrified.

The last thing I remember is being too drowsy to run away.

What kind of woman would do this to herself anyway?

Ten, nine, eight, seven, six, five . . .

5.

I awoke several hours later, seemingly alive, with a helmet wrapped around my head and swollen eyes, and immediately puked.

I was given apple juice in a paper cup, a saltine cracker, and the mean nurse who would take me home. It was a package deal.

She was twenty-four-hours inclusive.

Nurse Ratched eyed me with clear resentment.

She was older even than I and looked at me as if I was a foolish and frivolous female.

Ratched clearly had done this many times before and did not

approve of "rich bitches who lie." She coldly washed the dried blood from around my eyes.

Blasé, she had seen it all.

She was disdainful.

She knew how shallow I was.

We spoke little and as soon as her shift was up, she left me alone with my face.

This new face was black-and-blue. These new eyes were swollen. The punishment was severe.

I had earned this suffering and had even spent money on it.

6.

I informed the office that I was on vacation.

"Where?" they said.

"Hades," I answered, and they laughed.

And so it came to pass that the turban was taken off, the staples removed, stitches pulled, blood gone, the face refreshed at a price too dear to explain.

Did I look better?

I guess so.

I returned from this "vacation" not with a tan but with yellow and light blue streaks, and anyway, those who didn't know the truth knew I was a workaholic—so where had I been?

And so I made an announcement: "Guys, I had a face-lift." No one seemed surprised.

I went public and in and out of every office on my floor. The responses predictably came out as follows:

"Oh, you didn't need it."

"You were and are so beautiful."

"You look ten years younger."

You can count on these lies.

———————

But with this healing and this extra seven years of nothingness came this inexplicable feeling of "Why not try more? Why not try to please this spiteful x8 magnifying mirror? Why not be consistently dissatisfied with my appearance and other age-old parts?"

Every wrinkle would obsess me.

I looked at myself ten times a day.

I was known to bend over to peek into a side-view mirror of a stranger's car.

It seemed to me that one side of my face looked younger than the other.

And so I finally understood the aging Hollywood star who said, "This is my profile shot. Left side only."

7.

But the truth came in the pudding one Friday.

A temporary assistant named Violette, who of course had purple punk hair to match her name and tattoos and string bracelets all signifying some revolutionary cause, was assigned to me.

It wasn't until the end of the day that I noticed she had a gold ring in her lip. This tribal assistant, twenty years old, was also into alteration. Which to me signified that we had something precious in common.

"Violette," I said. "You did a great job today and I'm sorry I worked you so hard. What do you do usually?" I asked.

She said she was in her last year of college and that she hoped to devote her life to saving species whose extinction would herald the end of the universe. Fish were dying—amphibians, plants. The streams were getting too warm. The planet was belly-up.

"You know," I said to her, "I was part of the March on Washington in 1963. I made some of the posters."

"Oh," she said, thinking possibly I was involved in Lincoln's assassination.

We chatted about birds, and plants, and fish in danger. I told her fish were low in calories.

Violette was vested in the future.

"Oh, you're an honest kid," I said. "You tell it like it is. How old, Violette, do you think I am?"

She thought, unfazed. "You remind me of my mother. I don't know—sixty?"

"Close enough," I said, devastated. I was fifty-seven that very week.

8.

So then who was I fooling, really?

The taxi driver knew I was not with child and the child knew, even with my new face, that I was like her mother.

"Violette," I said, "would you ever have a face-lift?"

Twirling her lip ring with her tongue, she thought and said, "By the time I'm that old, there probably won't even be a planet."

"Do you feel good about yourself?" I asked.

"Yes," she said. "Because I feel badly for the world, that helps me feel good about myself."

"I guess so," I said. She was selfless and I was selfish.

Violette packed up to leave and went off to save the world.

I rouged and powdered my face with a little more passion than usual.

Did I feel better pulled and still numb? Yes and no.

Yes, for the camouflage of losing make-believe time.

No, because who was I fooling, really?

And yet, disturbingly, before I left the office, I called my dermatologist, Dr. Green.

"I need some refreshment," I said to the nurse. "Botox or whatever else she has. I think I have a new crevice on the right side of my lip."

"Let me see if Dr. Green can take you—hold on," she said. Then, "Dr. Green's got something new for you. She'd like you to try it. Can you come right away?"

"Yes. I can be there in twenty if I can get a cab."

"The doctor will wait."

———————

And so I jumped into a cab. It jolted and jerked. I didn't even pretend a pregnancy. I told the driver I had a bad back.

He asked me what I did for a living. Once upon a time they asked me if I was an actress. . . . Exhausted, I said, "I'm in real estate."

He looked in the mirror. "I thought you were an actress," he said.

It was worth it! I thought. *Look who I fooled!* I imagined all the beauties he thought I might have looked like.

And then he said, "I know who you are. You're Judge Judy."

I gulped.

"You really are Judge Judy, aren't you?" he insisted.

"I'm not," I said.

"You are."

"No, really, I'm not."

"All right," he said, "but I know the truth. . . ." He smiled, knowingly.

The verdict was out. I was fooling nobody. I looked like Judge Judy.

9.

Did I feel better about myself? Well, I was alive.

But the bottom line was that I heard a metronome ticking in my head that I had never heard before.

Maybe Dr. Baker had implanted it.

And maybe Dr. Green had wound it up.

Or maybe I was just plain crazy.

Time, time, time.

I rushed into the dermatologist's office. I couldn't wait for the new fix.

I would try it,

No matter how much it cost,

No matter how much it hurt,

Fooling no one.

Chills in the Hot Sun

HER PLANE was early. She never could adjust to the 8 a.m. flight from New York that arrived for lunch in L.A. anyway. It always seemed that she was a time traveler trying to buy up hours. And now that she arrived even earlier, she felt unsettled. She disembarked at the Peninsula Hotel, dropped her bag, and rushed to the rooftop. She ordered Tonic FluTea just in case, and leaned back in her chair. It had been raining in New York and so she brazenly faced the L.A. sun to bake her face, forgetting the skin doctor's admonition. How could anything that felt so good cause cancer? Warm was good. Cold was cancer.

He sat next to her. "Do you mind?" he said.

"I'm waiting for someone. My boss, to be exact," she said.

"Can I sit here 'til then?" he asked.

"I guess," she answered. "Why not?"

"I noticed you in the lobby."

"Noticed what?"

"That you were beautiful," he said.

"I'm hardly beautiful, and anyway, I'm old enough to be your mother."

"I like my mother."

She laughed. "Oedipus or incest? Take your pick."

"Either."

"I'm waiting for my boss, so don't be silly."

"Like what?"

"Like flirting with me."

"I'm not flirting with you. I'm telling you what I saw that was beautiful and it was you."

Chills in the hot sun; so odd; goose bumps. And so they chatted about this and that. Pizza versus cheeseburgers. Shakespeare and Ibsen. Green tea versus coffee. Ambien and Sonata. Sleep and sleepless. Now and never. He was a writer. She worked in television. He was divorced twice, no kids. She was married, one kid. He was forty-four.

"Oh, my God, forty-four," she said. "Change your seat." They laughed so loudly they disturbed a famous agent, hateful, but famous. Famous because hateful. And she smiled at him, this young, blind Romeo.

"I like your smile," he said.

"Veneers," she quipped. "They cost a fortune."

Time passed. Time always passes. *Tempus fugit.* Her boss called to change lunch until tomorrow. She could have taken a later plane. It was four. It was five. It was eight in real time—travel. Her nose burned.

"My nose is burning," she said. "I've got to go. Gotta go. I'm moist, my friend, well-buttered and baked," she said. "I'm on New York time."

"What room are you in?" he asked.

"Oh, please, little boy."

"What room, big girl?"

"Truthfully," she said, "I don't know. They give you this plastic key and you're supposed to remember. I never do. Darling, my room is my business. Frankly, you'd be disappointed anyway. Trust me. But it's been flattering to talk to you, engaging, even joyful."

"Joyful? You sound like Santa Claus," he said.

"Mrs. Claus," she said, "she's my age." She got up to leave. She brushed by him. And felt warmed by more than the sun.

Everything appeared to be in slow motion. She'd used that technique in her films to make a point. Her body blushed, or was it simply the remaining heat from the fading sun?

"I'm in room five fifty-two," he said as he got up to leave. "Five-five-two, Madame Beautiful."

"Prince Charming, don't expect a call. Though you are a darling young thing and I'm charmed to the nth."

At the front desk she handed her rectangular plastic key to the arched and plucked eye-browed concierge with a jacket labeled JACQUES JASPER.

"Ah, Ms. Dawson, how lovely to have you back at the Peninsula."

"Yes, Jacques Jasper, lovely to be here. Jacques or is it Jasper?"

"Jacques Jasper, Madame Dawson, I use both."

"Jacques Jasper, could you please tell me my room number? With these plastic things I always forget."

"Yes, Ms. Dawson, and how lovely you look tonight. Your room number is five fifty-three. Five-five-three, a beautiful room recently renovated. Have a lovely evening and enjoy your stay."

"Thank you, Jasper. I mean. Jacques. Silly me, sorry, Jacques Jasper." She waved good-bye, key in hand. And she entered the elevator—alone—and smiled to herself as she circled the 5 button several times round and then pressed it with her perfectly polished index finger. And the elevator door closed.

Heartbreak

ONE DAY they'll have a machine that shows a broken heart—an EKG of love gone astray. The printout will show the tear, and the doctor will say to the man or woman on the examining table, "Ah, I see your heart was broken at about seventeen or eighteen years of age." And you'll simply say, "Yes."

Last weekend I ran into a kid I knew slightly from around town—sweet faced and earnest. We seemed to arrive at the Starbucks at the same time many times. He had a beautiful girlfriend. She was the kind of local girl who had movie-star looks without even trying. I used to see him with her, staring over their frappé straws, looking deeply into each other's eyes. Sweet love. Young love. Evoking in me a kind of aching memory for never-again.

"Where's your girlfriend?" I asked.

"Oh," he said. "Brittany? We don't go out anymore."

"Ouch," I said. "Why not?" (The inevitable line at Starbucks was scarcely moving.)

"Well," he answered, "she went off to college and fell for some guy the first week."

"How awful," I said. "I'm so sorry."

"Yeah," he replied. "She dumped me!" (He ordered a venti caramel mocha latte.)

I had figured these two for the inevitable small-town dance-from-high-school sweethearts to side-by-side grave sites.

"How'd ya find out?" I asked the bereaved man-boy.

"Her girlfriend."

"You mean she never told you herself?" (I ordered a decaf misto with skim milk.)

"Nope, she never told me."

"How long were you together?"

"From sophomore year to graduation—two and a half years."

"Did you try to call her and get her to explain?"

"I tried," he said, "but she never answered my calls. She even returned the heart necklace and the belt buckle. No note. Nothing."

"That happened to me once," I said.

"You get over it?" he asked.

"Sure," I said. "It takes a while." I was lying.

You see, this is what I knew. I knew this boy would never get over this girl. Never, ever. Years later, marriage, kids, job travails and successes, family losses and triumphs—suddenly, a certain strain of music or a starlit night—these uninvited moments would bring back the pain of his broken heart and it would never heal. Unrequited love causes a nick forever in whatever pretend armor you wear. A broken heart can pierce the strongest of protective devices.

Poor kid, I thought. He started to pay at the pickup counter. I said, "Hey, let me pay for your venti caramel mocha latte."

"No, thanks." He smiled sadly.

"Please," I said. "It's the least I can do."

He said no, sweetly, and paid for this overpriced variation on a coffee theme.

———

One day science will discover this permanent now-invisible scar. They'll see it on some new kind of machine and point it out to the patient.

It will be an incidental finding.

Expensive Clothes

Expensive clothes never meant much to Priscilla Grimmler.

She suffered from Post-traumatic Stress Poverty, known currently in psychiatric circles as PTSP.

For in truth, Priscilla had grown up in abject poverty. The clothes she owned then were scarce, few, and simply for cover-up and of necessity.

All as cheap as cheap could be.

Yet now in adulthood she was the acknowledged queen of rags to riches.

She was loaded.

Millions of dollars surrounded her, and her business acumen made all recognize her as a successful multimillionairess, and very much so.

Yet Priscilla persisted in caring little for jewels or expensive garb—always looking for markdowns and bargains.

She could certainly afford fur.

She preferred faux.

And not for any love of animals.

Priscilla was a T.J.Maxx, Target, Costco kind of gal.

Buses not limos, giving small tips only to the extremely obliging,

Loving bargain clothing and cheap jewels and plastic shoes, all simply necessary objects to her. Nothing more.

———————

And then one day she made the business acquaintance of a fashion guru who would require her to go to investor events where fancy designer clothes would show that money matters.

They, together, would bottle a designer fragrance, costing pennies and netting a fortune.

Adding millions to millions,

This scent for cents.

It was necessary to oblige this grande dame and wear elegant attire, for Priscilla's continued job success in Dubai would be enhanced by making nice to these richly adorned fashionistas.

———————

Prissy, as her few friends called her, found herself in a dilemma.

She had to dress up for what she called, euphemistically, "many balls," as she would have to attend events where the whiff detected would be embraced by the cognoscenti and smell aloud worldwide.

———————

So Prissy found an obliging personal shopper and closed her eyes as Brenda from Bergdorf (a store known for its markups) outfitted her.

She was in emotional pain, remembering her impoverished childhood. In no time at all, racks were rolled in and Prissy was outfitted in the finest of silks and fabrics, whose cost made her swoon.

Pointed shoes that pinched, dresses with famous-name labels, fur that cried "ouch," and bags that smelled of leather.

Hours later, exhausted from adornment, Priscilla left the store garbed.

A stranger to herself.

She stopped for a jelly doughnut advertised as a two-for-one Dunkin' special and then rode the bus home forlorn, overloaded with boxes and bags to avoid any delivery charges.

The next evening, after a sleepless night tortured by dreams of want, she dressed in Versace to kill, jeweled with real Harry Winston gems, hobbling in five-inch Manolo Blahniks, and left her apartment to meet with the contacts of the prime fashionista of the Middle Eastern world.

No sooner had she stepped out of her apartment, hoping to pull it off, when she was besieged by an inexplicable madness to pull it off. To pull it all off.

She rocked back and forth in her stilettos and suddenly threw them, leaving herself barefoot in the lobby of her rent-controlled building.

Then she hysterically tore at her dress, shredding it. She pulled off her jewels, pearls, and rings. She flung the contents of her purse all over the lobby floor, subway *tokens and single dollar bills, leaving her in her Walmart bra and panties—residual garments that were memories of her former self.*

The doorman, Caesar, seeing this display, rushed to escort his almost naked tenant upstairs.

Alarmed, he covered her in his uniform jacket (that misspelled Caesar as Cesar) and delivered her into her hallway where she shivered and shuddered and promised him a bigger tip for next Christmas.

"Don't leave me," she begged as she gave him her bags of new clothes, jewels, and rich-lady paraphernalia.

It was a bonanza for Caesar. Forget that she never tipped me last Christmas, *he thought.*

———————

Priscilla fell into her bed exhausted.

She sent for a Domino's pepperoni pizza, canceled the scent event, and apologized by phone to the accomplice, who was kept waiting and was furious about the sudden turn of events.

Priscilla soon fell into a deep sleep in the embrace of her JCPenney sheets and comforter.

The bed was covered in pepperoni. She was happy— this poor little rich girl. A very poor once and very rich little girl now.

———————

And thus the diagnosis of Post-traumatic Stress Poverty, P.T.S.P., code 7321, made it into the physician's handbook of diagnoses, reimbursable under some insurance plans and known colloquially as P.G.P., the Priscilla Grimmler Phenomenon.

As for personal dresser Brenda, she continued to dress those who concurred, the scent-de-cents never was whiffed, and Caesar remained a doorman for three decades with his name misspelled on his uniform. He would often recall to workmates the strip scene of a certain Miss Grimmler from apartment 2C, who lived in the back of the building.

———

As for Priscilla herself, she continued to dress as cheaply as she could, seeking sales and markdowns while amassing more millions over the decades and eventually dying, as the rich and poor will do.

Priscilla left all her money to doorman Caesar for saving her dignity during her foray into expensive.

Her will read: "I am my child forever.

My child is me."

And then it said,

"And to Cesar" (misspelled), "my fortune.

Thank you, Cesar, for preserving that poor little girl on that dreadful night so long ago."

The Elephant in the Room

She hated celebratory parties, social events, and
  dinners with friends,
As she always wanted to say
Something unspeakable out loud.
Some thought she was shy, a loner
But really, in this case, she was
Dangerous.

———————

Did Marty know Maureen was
Sleeping with his best friend Maurice?
Did Alice (who just got into Yale)
Know she was not Alexandra's
Birth child?
Did Bart know his wife, Betty,
Lied about her age
When she married him
And still didn't tell the truth
Some five years later?

And so it would happen
That keeping these troublesome secrets to herself
Would keep her absent mostly.

———————

And when her last invitation
To dinner with Frieda and Frank (to see slides of their
*   twenty-fifth anniversary in New Delhi)*
Arrived at the office
By messenger no less—
She simply RSVP'd
"Regrets. Sorry."
Because Frank was going to leave
Frieda for her very self the very next day. Poor, poor
*   Frieda.*
And so she preferred not to
Break bread and engage in phony laughter, or forced
*   chatter*
About the thrill of riding elephants,
For had she gone,
She would be the infidelity elephant in the room.
For she was not only an absent "party pooper"
But obviously,
Absolutely,
Quite
Dangerous.

Separate Bedrooms for Marcia and Larry

MARCIA AND Larry Leinsdorf had been married for thirty-one years this past June. Many considered it an ideal marriage, and as far as marriages go, it was ideal—if you get my drift. They had long ago stopped fighting over details and trying to make life perfect. As hot and steamy left the bedroom, a cool calm took over their relationship. It wasn't that there wasn't love; it was just that it was love redefined. They were the best of friends, completed each other's stories, knew the punch line of each other's jokes, and both liked fresh borscht with floating scallions (which were hard to catch) made by Corazonista, the Brazilian maid who had been with them for thirty of their thirty-one years.

The Leinsdorfs had made four children, all boys, and given the way that some of their friends' kids turned out, they considered themselves lucky. The boys were moderately kind to their parents, called them occasionally, and sent cards on Mother's Day, Father's Day, and birthdays. Often late, but they never forgot them totally. After weathering millions of dirty diapers, etc., rashes, etc., childhood illnesses, etc., college acceptance angst, etc., homework, etc., graduation, etc., and daughters-in-law that were not up to snuff, etc., etc., etc., Larry and Marcia accepted the fact that, in almost all circumstances, they had been there and they had done that and that was just perfectly fine with them.

Their evenings were the only thing that shattered the safe monotony of their committed monogamy. At nighttime they lost their well-earned synchronicity. They could not orchestrate Marcia's menopausal nighttime sweats with Larry's aging prostate's frequent trips to pee. And so, like a seesaw, each blamed the other for their own lack of sleep. Their marriage was at the tipping point. As Marcia turned down the air conditioner's temperature, Larry would awaken. When she threw off the covers he said it startled him and anyway he was always cold. "I'm freezing," he said. "I'm sweating, Larry, like a pig," she said. She was hot; he was frigid. Marcia reminded Larry that each time he got up to pee she had just fallen asleep and could not get back to sleep and, alas, when she finally did fall asleep, he would get up and pee again. It went something like this:

MARCIA: You woke me three times.

LARRY: No, you woke me three times.

MARCIA: You always have to pee and the floorboards squeak.

LARRY: I peed only twice last night.

MARCIA: Three, Larry, three times. Can't you tiptoe to the bathroom?

LARRY: I do tiptoe. I try. And by the way, you are always tugging my side of the bed when you violently throw off the blanket because you're so hot.

MARCIA: Well, I am hot, Larry.

LARRY: Well, I can't help it when nature calls.

Now, since their youngest son, Jonathan, had gone off to law school, their downsized apartment had an extra bedroom. This was a tempting option and Marcia didn't know how to tell Larry,

but she wanted Jonathan's bed and bedroom for herself—
desperately.

One night she broke the news to Larry:

> MARCIA: Larry, you wouldn't mind if I tried Jonathan's
>   room. His old bed is close to the air conditioner and
>   it has twelve thousand BTUs.

This information was actually comforting to Larry, who had
himself thought of moving into Jonathan's room—though he
thought it was too far from the bathroom.

> LARRY: You mean separate bedrooms?
> MARCIA: Let's try it.
> LARRY: How do we tell our friends?
> MARCIA: No one will ask.
> LARRY: What about your mother?
> MARCIA: Trust me, she knows about long marriages and
>   separate beds.
> LARRY: I'd rather no one else knew.
> MARCIA: It's not as if we do anything in bed anyway, Larry.
> LARRY: But no one knows.
> MARCIA: No one cares.
> LARRY: I guess. Are we still married then, or roommates?
> MARCIA: We're married roommates.
> LARRY: Okay, it's between us. Don't tell the kids.
> MARCIA: Of course not.

So, secretly, Marcia moved into her son Jonathan's room. The
room had the scent of her last child; the distant smell of
the marijuana he smoked, the too-sweet scent of his aftershave.
She could sense his presence in the smell of this pillow—her new
pillow. Moreover, Jonathan's air conditioner was perfect. It didn't
freeze over when she needed a cool breeze in late December.

And so, the Leinsdorfs began to get a good night's sleep for the first time in years. It was her menopause versus his prostate and they both won. Larry loved his new freedom. He didn't feel guilty when he had erotic dreams or touched himself. He learned the pleasure of sleeping on the diagonal with covers that stayed still through the night. In addition, he did not have to walk on tiptoe to pee. He enjoyed the sound of a gentle stomp on the squeaky floorboards. Marcia, on the other hand and in the other room, slept naked with the air conditioner on . . . and she slept like a baby.

So, this is how the Leinsdorfs continued to be the ideal couple. And one night Larry said to Marcia as they bid their adieus, "Now that I can sleep, I love you even more." And Marcia said, "I love you more too, Larry Leinsdorf." Marcia patted Larry's prominent bald spot and said, "Pleasant dreams, Larry." And they kissed like children on the lips without tongues.

From *Cosmo* to *Ms.*

I WANTED TO be a *Cosmo* girl. I dreamed of plunging necklines and men falling at my feet. Always sorry that my breasts were too small and that my nipples seemed inverted, I maximized by bra what nature had minimized. There was no Amazon overnight delivery then. I rushed my *Cosmo* delivery, five days from the post office—a push-up-and-out bra. (Does anyone use the post office anymore?)

I played seductive. High I.Q. Barnard degree be damned. I loved that I could bewitch them, those unsuspecting, dreary male work fellows, and turn them into amours as I played the office vixen. I would be lying if I said I didn't also dream of Helen Gurley Brown calling me up for a photo op. I was young, pretty, and game. Cover-girl potential (except for my tits). I read *Cosmo* as biblical text. I lived by its psalms. I followed. I was pretty-girl provocateur—buying attention with a too-short skirt.

How could I?

Well, I did!

Don't judge me unless you were there way back then and wanting a fair shot.

Take Mr. Delore, a married man about forty. I enjoyed making his temperature rise. "Yes, Mr. Delore," I would say. "I'll pick up your tuna melt sandwich . . . anything else?" I'd milk the pause while sliding my office chair in his direction and watch him adjust his now growing-too-tight pants. I adored the notion that at any given moment some office jerk might be jerking off to me—false temptress trying to advance in the Land of Media. Flitting about town, buying skintight jeans and revealing angora sweaters that plunged and itched. Plunge won over itch. I was at the first step of the staircase and I wanted to climb to the highest floor. Helen Gurley Brown assured me this was the way to the top.

After Barnard I went on to Yale to get an MFA in directing at the Yale School of Drama. What to do after graduation? A girl had to be married in those times. Being single and trying to make it on your own meant there was something wrong with you. So I married a tie and button-down shirt I had known briefly at Yale. Why did I marry him? Just because, and not ever for love. What was a 1960s woman to do if she wanted to travel and see the world and also didn't earn enough to rent an apartment alone in the big city?

Married and seductive. Unavailable—yet available to you, boss man—and dangerous. I was the siren with a cause.

Or so I thought. What did I know?

Yet outside, somewhere, there were women marching for equal rights. They were playing songs, but not for me. Of this I was sure. I was on a *Cosmo* climb. Ambitious with wiles. I enjoyed being young forever. I was a Gurley by Helen. There were midnight calls from married men from corner phone booths. They couldn't sleep, they said, dreaming of me. Their hands likely on their crotches. I scored with them without them scoring. Well, mostly. I listened obediently to their romantic overtures. So what if I fooled around?

Oh, those late-night calls. Interruptions for more change. "Time's up," said a real operator, interjecting during a passionate (one-sided) late-night call from, say, Married Man #3, Tubby. He was the boss or next in line to be next in line. Tubby would put in more change. *Hey, Tubster,* I thought, *never too much of a young thing?* You paid with change for calls then. He added quarters—kerplunk—into the pay phone. (Guess they don't make those pay phones anymore either.) But there is always a marker that never dates—young women and middle-aged married men. To you, Helen Gurley Brown, and because of you, I could cycle through these married men after brief encounters.

I continued to see women outside marching for equal rights and I wondered, what were these women fighting for? What did I care for equality or rights? I was to be the "me" of then—forever.

Or was I? I was standing still. Now twenty-seven. Never promoted. Five years after college. Bored. Used. Married. Restless. Going nowhere. Maybe to bed—my interpretation of wicked equality. That was all I knew. The bureaucracy dominated by men objectified me into a leg-spreading mannequin. And for this wooden performance, I performed on call. Smart college girl! To men in superior positions, I was inferior. I was a call-her girl. Call girl? But why not? Housewife not. Wife not. Career not really. So what was I? Gurley Brown, I trusted you. But were you just of the moment? And would the moment last days to years to decades? Well, not for me, it didn't. Life intervened.

After three years of playing the *Cosmo* card, drinks, etc., with married men, I felt a bit weary. Where was I going and who would let me go there? I divorced my dictator Yale husband. Gave him the furniture; I took the posters. He made me feel as if I was a loser and not a real woman. After all, I balked at taking his shirts to the laundry and I couldn't cook. He insisted on homemade dinners and clean dishes before I left for work. "Can't I wash the coffee cups later?" I would ask. "No," he would say. "Now." Worse, I was a lefty and couldn't sew on his shirt buttons if they popped. He scolded me for asking the tailor to sew them on. "Women sew," he said.

Maybe I wasn't a woman after all. I had to prove to myself I had what it took to be like other women, so I deliberately got pregnant before I left him. How ridiculous was that? Intentionally not using my diaphragm. I hated him and was not ready for motherhood, especially if he was to be the father. (At least I had proved I was fertile, so I was a woman.) I then had an illegal abortion, hemorrhaging a week later and nearly dying—bleeding and winding up in a New York City emergency room.

Days passed, body wounds healed, but my mind was sore. And I began to wonder . . . why was I never *really* promoted? Why was it illegal to not want a pregnancy? Where was I going? Why did these guys call me panting at 12:53 a.m.? Why didn't I have the balls to hang up? Didn't they think I slept? And why did I feel compelled to go along with these calls? Because, I thought, as Helen had taught me, sex was power, submission my passport. But the truth was I was traveling nowhere. Okay, maybe down. And too far. I was depressed. They gave me Valium. It made me drowsy but stopped the tears and the sense of irrelevance.

What made me give up Miss for Ms.? Helen for Gloria? Was it the blood of the abortion? The garish night in that office building? Being thrown on the mattress with three other trembling sinners? Was it the abortionist who asked for three hundred dollars in cash up front? While my feet were in makeshift stirrups, he stuck me with some poker with his right hand while drinking a Tab diet soda with his left. This quasi doctor who spoke little English came out afterward and told us, "You have successfully killed your babies." I started to cry. The three of us held each other's trembling hands. Then there was the doctor who treated me a week later for hemorrhaging in a legitimate New York hospital. He had given me birth control pills and then one bloody month later was nonethical enough to get my phone number off of my medical chart and call me and ask me on a date, laughing that if I was taking the new pills, we'd be safe in bed. Ha-ha.

Miss for Ms.? Maybe it was the mindless fucking that went nowhere. Or the obligation of bringing Yale husband's shirts to the laundry. Or being scolded for dirty dishes.

Or was it that one day, carelessly throwing my paycheck in

my bag, when I arrived home to find surprisingly that the check was not mine. I always looked at the amount because it was hard to believe I could be paid for what I loved, even though it was not much at the time. Somehow a male colleague's check had been put in my envelope. We had the same job title. I worked on even more shows per month than he did. The difference— the amount on his check was twice mine. I steamed and fretted and realized who I was. I was a woman in the early '70s. Were men worth more?

All of this made me cry. All of this made me angry. I wanted a life. I wanted my colleague's check. I wanted that male power. I wanted to be equal. I wanted to play ball in a man's ballpark. I felt doomed by a cunt. But then, as I was sinking, I said to myself, "No way, José."

So how did I cross over the bridge? Why did I give up my tight sweaters for comfy? Why did I embrace sisterhood? Why did I join up and attend marches, crying ERA?

I heard the words of Bella and Gloria. I listened attentively, and they said I was not an object. I was not to be subjugated. That I should get equal pay. That I was a Ms., not a Miss (or a tempfuck replacing a Mrs.). I read Gloria, who said, "Any woman who chooses to engage like a full human being . . . she will need her sisterhood." Sisterhood. Hmm. Women bonding with women. Women who wanted equality. I was soon to be a rebel. I wanted what I deserved, and I deserved a right to my own body, equal rights, equal pay.

My seducing days ended. I stopped bringing coffee and as if they read my mind, the guys in the office stopped asking—for everything. And so part two of my life would begin in earnest. I would make a deliberate turn from *Cosmo* to *Ms.* as I began to idolize sisterhood. Nevertheless, I thanked Helen Gurley Brown for the hot ride down a crooked path. Had I not stumbled, and hurt so bad, I might never have known. I turned the page, finally, and so it would be that I learned how to spell F-E-M-I-N-I-S-T and to be one. No late-night calls, no flirtations, no courting for success. Earning what was my due. Smart, talented, aggressive, girly to womanly power. Me.

And why not? It was the march I was meant to march in. It was just a slow walk at first—to get the drum, find the sticks, and feel the beat, and finally put it all together. To march. I've got what it takes, I told myself, without wiles, short skirts, and plunging necklines. I reached out to other women, young women. Women in my predicament or those who soon would be.

Powwow rumble.

Let me in, Woman Power.

I'm in.

Time passes. The march goes on.

And even though the climb, for me, has never been easy,

Women have power.

Go, Girl, go.

Chocolate Chemo

AS ANNA lay dying—

We laughed our heads off when the ice cream sprinkles got stuck on her nose. The cancer had spread from her ovaries to her lungs and then to her kidneys. She had refused treatment. Her chemo of choice, she said, was the Mister Softee I would bring, with the scattered sprinkles.

"Don't I look silly?" she asked, wiping her chocolate nose with the crumpled tissue she always had on her night table.

"Yes, silly," I answered. "But beautiful."

And after a pause, "Was it worth it?" I asked her. "This life thing."

We would often turn from giggling to philosophizing about life.

And she thought for a minute and said, "I don't think I laughed enough." We laughed hysterically at that. "I think I sweated too much of the small stuff," she said, laughing, "like burning a soufflé."

"You're a great cook," I said.

"I was," she corrected me, and then added, "I don't think I knew it would end, this life thing. But most importantly"—she smiled wickedly—"I don't think I got laid enough."

"Oh, please," I remember saying. "When the goo is gone the glue is gone." And we laughed again.

"You can buy that stuff," she said, "silly child." She was two decades older than I was then.

"Are you scared of dying?" I asked. Death had openly entered the room, barring euphemism.

"When you get to my age," she said softly, "you know more people on the other side then you do here. It gets lonely."

"Do you believe there's an other side?" I asked.

"Of course not!" she said, summoning strength. And for some reason we both found her response hilariously funny.

She was eighty-five. I hoped to be like her when my time came. I enjoyed the rehearsal. I loved to visit her these months before the end. A dry run? A dress rehearsal? Maybe. Would I have her charm and courage? Would someone slightly behind me in time rehearse with me? Anna was precious. The battery clock near her bed didn't utter a sound but I heard its chimes.

"I love you, Anna," I said.

I would see her the same time next Sunday. "You don't have to come," she reminded me. "Many friends can't bear to see me this way."

"The way you is, is the way you is," I answered. She corrected my grammar. I kissed her cool cheek good-bye.

She asked me to pick up the chocolate Mister Softee again next week. I said I would. And her voice followed me down the stairs.

"And maybe you could bring some extra sprinkles? The multi-colored ones. They disappear so quickly."

The Giant Named Tourette's

I COULD NEVER love anyone more. He was my little boy, David. I never knew he would fight Goliath. And yet he did. It was a giant that I would finally learn was named Tourette's. Tourette's would crush and stomp on all dreams of normalcy. Tourette's would disturb quiet, sunny times with a thunderous clap. Tourette's would enter without invitation and was the dybbuk that would overcome my relatively ruly child.

Tourette's came slowly at first. When David was two, I noticed continuous eye blinking, so I took him to the eye doctor. But in the office he didn't blink once. The doctor was unimpressed and suggested that David might have dry eyes. So I bought a humidifier. It didn't help at all. I then took him to some pediatric eye specialist who suggested cortisone drops. Those didn't work either. No one knew what was wrong. David would continue to blink somewhat inconsistently and excessively. Sometimes thirty times in succession and then not at all.

When he was about three, I noticed this peculiar raising of his right shoulder. He would raise it again and again, and touch his ear repeatedly. Then there were these low grunting noises, almost like throat clearing. None of these behaviors were predictable. They would explode and then recede. Some days they seemed to vanish and then they would hurricane in, as if a storm had possessed him.

Why couldn't he stop? Respectable pediatricians said that the throat clearing was possibly from tonsils that were too large. So we determined we would remove them come spring. The eye blinking they were convinced was dry eyes. As for the shoulder raising, the experts said it was transient. "Don't worry, Sheila," the doctors would say, "it's just a tic he'll outgrow." But it got worse. The tics, as they were called, continued and morphed into variations.

A new child psychiatrist, highly recommended, told me my long business trips might be making David nervous. He was an expert in child behavioral disorders and suggested that mothers' absences are much more significant than those of their husbands. Our pediatrician and this psychiatrist, the best that Park Avenue had to offer, concurred that I was most likely the root of David's excessive ticking. The doctors suggested I travel less for this job that I loved. But I never loved my job more than I loved David. If the tics would stop, I would be a stay-at-home mom. But somehow my husband and I didn't trust this theory. The ailment seemed independent of my work and I was almost always in attendance when it came to David—with little sleep, red-eye travel, present at every parent meeting.

One night, unable to sleep, I carefully watched video footage of David's last birthday party—he was six. I noticed eye-raising twitches and throat clearing. I wondered if I had forgotten the three-times-a-day drops, although I was compulsive about them being given exactly on time. What did I do wrong? Tell me.

And then, as if things weren't bad enough, the school headmaster called, stating, somewhat confrontationally, that David was rudely spitting in class.

"Sorry," I said. "I'll talk to him."

Spitting in homeroom, spitting in reading, spitting in math. Oh, dear.

"David," I said. "You must stop that spitting. You just must."

He slammed the door to his room so hard the freshly painted ceiling plaster fell. Why couldn't he stop?

But it continued—the spitting, the grunting, the throat clearing, the eye blinking—adding wrist twisting and eyebrow raising. I was beside myself. Should I quit this delicious job?

The school called and threatened again. He cannot stay if he continues spitting—that was the headmaster's message.

"Can you stop this spitting, David?" I said one night, exhausted.

"I tried and I can't stop," he said and burst into tears.

"What do you think makes you grunt? Is your throat sore?" I pleaded.

"I don't grunt. What's a grunt anyway?"

Was it possible he was somehow unaware?

"Leave me alone. I'm not going to school anymore. The kids make fun of me. They call me Chief Spit Face."

"They shouldn't do that. Try your best to stop spitting," I said, "and maybe they won't make fun."

"I can't, Mom. I want to and even if I did try, I don't know when I'm going to do it."

I put a sobbing boy to bed. I looked at his sixth birthday video again late that night. Was it possible that he didn't know what was actually going on in his own body? The party had been at Jeremy the Clown's workshop. These kids were so cute in their hats, blowing their paper bugles. I watched David on the tape, replaying the party again and again from a thick cassette. It was 1986. I wanted to watch him carefully. I had a toothache anyway and I couldn't sleep. The dentist was set for tomorrow.

The birthday boy sang first. "Happy birthday to me." (David would clear his throat.) "Happy birthday to me." (David would giggle.) "Happy birthday to me, I'm David!" (David would blink his eyes.) "Happy birthday to me." And then he spit. All the kids laughed. Could it be that David didn't even know he was spitting?

I wept to my husband. "What is wrong? What did I do?"

"Nothing," he said. "Don't blame yourself. He's my son too. You're a great mom."

"What should we do?" I asked, crying.

"Maybe we should remove his tonsils now," he suggested.

"Yes," I agreed.

"Maybe all this is related," my husband said.

"Yes, yes," I said.

The next morning David refused to go to school. I called the pediatrician, known to her kid patients as Dr. Susie.

I was crying. "There is something wrong with David, like a paralysis or a seizure or something."

"Sheila, lots of kids do this. It will pass," she said. And, alas, she was a woman—a working woman with grown children. Did they twitch and spit and grunt? Did it pass, I wondered?

The babysitter came early and I rushed to the dentist. Root canal. I had to do it now. I waited in the office. I leafed through *Family Circle* magazine. It was full of recipes and cooking tips that I would never need. And an article on Tourette's. I thought that was when funny-looking people said dirty words in public. That was all I knew.

I read the article carelessly. Suddenly I was riveted by a section that gave a list for diagnosing Tourette's: two motor tics. I thought, eye blinking, spitting. One verbal tic. Hmm—throat clearing and grunting. I dropped the magazine. *David has Tourette's. Goddamn it, David has Tourette's!* I tore the list from the magazine and rescheduled the dental appointment. The tooth hardly hurt. I was determined to bring this information home. Hey, expensive doctors! Hey, book-writing pediatricians! Hey, headmaster at a fancy prep school! Did you ever hear about Tourette's?

And so began . . . The Tourette's Game. Neurologists, doctors who concurred, pills to try. Why me's and sad outbursts. I was not always noble. Yet David was always in front, brave with the knowledge and forthright in acceptance. As if he said to himself, "I have Tourette's but Tourette's doesn't have me." David seemed relieved knowing he had a diagnosis and accepting that it was not within his control. He had always known that his tics were not malicious or deliberate. If he wanted to know anything, it was why they were there and where they had come from.

"Why does my body do what I don't want it to do?" he asked.

And so came useless explanations that I deemed suitable for a now seven-year-old. "A body sometimes messes up," I said. "And then it gets better. And the body's brain can be very very very smart." Or so I hoped that jumble would explain it. "You see, sometimes the body mixes up messages like getting the wrong mail."

He answered, "You're not making sense."

I wasn't making sense. I was there alone in Tourette's Land. I didn't really know the answer. There were no tools, no books, no videos. It was hard to explain to a child.

The spitting would stop eventually, replaced by nose scratching and face scrunching. The grunting lowered. Then came object touching and various milder versions of ADHD, OCD, and other concomitant symptoms. I learned from the experts, not then easily found in the field, that Tourettic symptoms change and replace old ones with new ones as they seize the neurological system. Medicines came mostly not approved for children. The medicine was try and see, and watch very carefully.

And so the symptoms would wax and wane. David would grow into them and out of them. Strangely, I found myself doing several imitative tics. I don't know how or why that happened. I would chew my lip and clear my throat involuntarily. On some subconscious level, maybe I was trying to lessen his symptoms by adopting them as my own. I read everything, went to meetings, enrolled him in various tests. I cried a lot.

But this is the point really. We were not alone. In 1885, Georges Gilles de la Tourette, a neurologist, had discovered a syndrome in schoolchildren in France that would be named after him. Today, symptoms of this disorder are seen in one out of every hundred schoolchildren. I could never thank this doctor enough.

An imperfect, challenged child gives one empathy and insights.

I'm not going all Pollyanna here. Nonetheless, I am somewhat grateful for the wisdom, though always furious at the price we paid.

David accepted tics and incorporated them into being who he was. Smart, wise, difficult. His own kid.

David is now all grown. The symptoms have subsided—except for an occasional grunt, well hidden and easily acceptable. But David happens to be one of the lucky ones. What to say? What to learn? Only 5 percent of people with Tourette's have coprolalia, which is yelling out unacceptable or forbidden words. The media has not done Tourette's justice. So be kind when someone involuntarily shouts out or twists and tics. Have pity—they can't help it. They have as much control over their actions as they do over the color of their eyes or their height. It's all just genetics determining this variety of sounds and configurations.

My boy is a hero. He is a success at work. He chases stray cats and seeks rescue dogs. His heart is easily touched and the tears spent in childhood make his empathy deep and personal, yet always reserved. He is the complex product of his unusual self.

No, I do not wish Tourette's on anyone. But life is not a bowl of cherries. I have grown to appreciate diversity in others and laugh out loud and long at the good things in life. I wanted David to be accepted like everyone else. I certainly did not want him to be bullied as he was. I learned from David that standing out, if you survive, can have its own applause. It makes you unique in a copycat world. It makes you see the possibilities in difference. The price is dear but exceptions nudge us forward.

———

David let me write this. I asked him if I could. Thanks, David.

For more information on Tourette's visit the Tourette Association of America at http://www.tourette.org/

Little Blue Pill

IT WAS odd, she thought, that Hyram would be working late for so many nights. After all, it wasn't tax season and May, June, and July were slow periods for Hy and his highly regarded CPA firm. But Anthea had been through other disappearing acts with Hy—often culminating in a lipstick smudge (not hers) on his shirt or a strange aroma of a perfume (not hers as well).

However, after forty years of marriage, Anthea accepted these occasional signs of peccadillos. She looked the other way. Yet alluded elusively to Hy that she knew what he knew that she knew and that both had decided to not know. To keep the order, to keep the peace, to keep the marriage going, and to avoid the infidelity card, they played the game.

Anthea would say, "Odd perfume-like smell in the house, Hy."

And Hy would reply, sniffing, "Maybe it's the dog shampoo— they always put too much perfume in those washes. Silly thing to do."

And then she would add, enjoying Hy's discomfort, "Did you know a dog's sense of smell is about twenty times stronger than a human's?" Anthea would say this not to change the topic, but to emphasize that she knew the true topic and to prove that she was not fooled by a smudge or a wafting aroma.

After Hy's shirts were laundered, Anthea was known to point out the troubling lipstick stain, saying casually, "Sweetheart, this smudge on your shirt. It's so low down—you can just tuck it in your pants." And then she would innocently ask, "Any important meetings today, darling?"

Hy would acknowledge this stain and would nod and say that the housekeeper Angelique's eyesight was simply failing. And Anthea would naïvely reply in a babyish voice, "But Angelique has perfect eyesight since she had her cataracts removed four years ago."

And so it would be that this tit for tat, or should we say tat for tits, would include variations on this dishonesty theme. But basically, no matter what they said, the façade was always the same.

Anthea, however, for all her tolerating of Hy's behavior, was not beyond direct revenge. She generally appeared to be a kind and dutiful wife. She was great as a grandmother and a devoted librarian at the local school. But she could also be spiteful and sinister.

One day while riffling through Hy's Gucci briefcase, the expensive one she had bought him for last Father's Day, turning the combination lock she had programmed herself (three to the left, nine to the right, four to the left), she found a fresh bottle of thirty blue Pfizer Viagra pills. Her friends bemoaned this thing called Viagra. Her neighbor Angie said it kept these old guys up but they had so much trouble bringing it down that this pharmaceutically assisted love play could take forever. She and Angie had both laughed, called it a fucking pill. And a fucking pill it was. It allowed these middle-aged men/husbands with protruding bellies not only to have occasional sex with their wives, but also to go hard after anything else that was ambitious and younger and available at the office.

The bottle label reported that Hy's pills had been refilled five times and there was one refill left. *Dearest Hy*, she thought. Four bottles used. Thirty pills in each. A hundred and twenty thrusts.

In what seemed to be less than a year? Her darling had scored a record number of one-shot possibilities. Even as young lovebirds, Anthea and Hy had never met those expectations.

And so Anthea schemed. She raced through the Internet to find a comparable looking blue pill. She finally found one called Meclizine, a pill known to stop seasickness and dizziness. She didn't think something so mild could hurt him permanently. Or did she? She did want Hy around. And so she got a prescription and filled it. She replaced the Viagra with thirty blue Meclizine, knowing for certain that Hy would be much too excited at his moments of need to ever notice the slight difference. This Meclizine used for seasickness would certainly prevent her Hy from rocking back and forth. She was pleased.

And so it would come to pass that Hy's late-night business meetings would decline. Hy would come home earlier. Together, they would binge various television series, and she even watched an occasional sporting event with him. She deviously smiled during these periods of pseudotogetherness. And when he would say, "Honey, I'm home," she would think, *The big rat*. And yet she would say, "Hi, sweetie, soup's on."

And one night, as they were celebrating their fortieth anniversary with their three children and their seven grandkids, their daughter, Roberta, held up a glass to toast her happy parents. And as the glasses were high, their daughter said, "To my great parents. Happily married for forty years. Role models." And then she asked her parents, "To what do you attribute this long-standing romance?"

At which point Hy grandly remarked, "There is only one Anthea. Only one who knows me so well and whom I will love forever."

And Anthea smiled and toasted, saying, " 'Love is not love which alters when it alteration finds.' " Shakespeare's complexity came in handy when at a loss for true words. And only Anthea and the Bard understood exactly what that quote meant.

Jeremy Hit Rock Bottom

I WENT TO a funeral today. It was for a child, a nineteen-year-old boy, my friend's difficult son. The police report said he had overdosed on cocaine and alcohol. He had fallen against a bathroom sink during a cocaine seizure and died in the emergency room of a public hospital. His heart stopped. Someone at the party he was at had dialed 911 too late and disappeared. These details were in the police report. This beautiful child was dead forever. We'll call him Jeremy. His mother, my good friend, we'll call her Grace, wept uncontrollably.

Six months earlier, after sending Jeremy to seven rehabs and AA, NA, and CA meetings—all to no avail—she had decided to throw Jeremy out of the house. She told me that he had exhausted her patience as well as her finances. Expensive rehab never worked. His "higher power" appeared to be his addictive personality. Grace had been told to let him hit rock bottom. She wept, curled up on my lap sobbing, whispering hoarsely that she had herself overdosed on the prevailing diagnosis of being unduly complicit in her son's addiction. She had been advised, wherever she sought help, that by sheltering him, she had been an enabler—and that she had allowed her son to continue his abuse. Her empathetic behavior was his downfall, or so she had been told. "I'm letting him go," she said one day, surprising me.

"That's what I've been told to do. I'm an enabler. I've been too passive—Jeremy has to hit the ground and get up. That's what they all say. I'm through aiding and abetting." She blamed herself. "I'm a fucking enabler, sorry to curse. I'm complicit, yes, I am. I'm making it worse by being so soft." That was Grace six months before the funeral.

Grace was now left with one child, her daughter—we'll call her Mandy. Mandy had not left her room. She refused to go to the funeral. Mandy had turned seventeen three days before her brother's death. I had known Mandy since she was six pounds and three ounces—a perfect baby girl. Then Mandy started having seizures and was later diagnosed at seven as epileptic. Grace and I went to many neurologists together. Finally, Mandy was put on several various medications and they seemed to mostly work. Her epileptic seizures were milder, and though slightly tremulous at times, Mandy led a relatively normal life. She was her high school's valedictorian, had a solicitous boyfriend, lots of girlfriends, and bragged outrageously over her Ivy stripes with early admission to Harvard.

Jeremy was another story. Handsome, funny, and—in spite of it all—sweet, but he had always been a difficult child. At an early age he was diagnosed with ADHD. Jeremy had tantrums, was completely disorganized, and totally unpredictable. Little things would set him off. Some doctors said he was bipolar, some said he had a mood disorder. Who knew? At thirteen he was smoking and drinking and lying about it. By fifteen he was doing drugs and stealing—taking alcohol, cigarettes, then ecstasy and soon speed. Nothing helped. Jeremy's father was remarried and Grace was unable to get her ex to help her with their only son. A single parent, a working mom, she went to meetings where she found like-minded mothers who had successfully taken a hard line with their kids. But this hard line was not foolproof. She knew that. But exasperated and running out of money and patience, she decided to untie her enabling and try the recommended tough love. "Out," she said to Jeremy. "Out!" She changed the locks. "If you can't come home clean," she said, "don't come back at all!" And when she slammed the door she felt uneasy but correct in her behavior. It had been advised.

Time passed. Grace hadn't heard from Jeremy for months. Not a word. She was worried sick, sleepless and fearful. She often held Mandy and they sobbed together night after night. Mandy wanted her brother home at any price. His cell phone rang unanswered. His friends, the few he had, had not heard a peep. "Mom, get him back," Mandy cried. Her seizures increased.

And then one evening, the phone call . . . "Mrs. Hanratty?"

"Yes, this is she."

"Is this Grace Hanratty?"

"Yes," she said.

"Are you the mother of Jeremy Hanratty?"

"Yes, yes," she said desperately. As the mother of a missing boy, she knew what was next.

"This is Sergeant Adams and I'm sorry to tell you . . ."

I held her hand at the cemetery. Jeremy was buried next to his adoring grandmother and grandfather. They had lived to eighty and eighty-five. Long lives. I wondered in my heart if Jeremy was responsible for his addiction. Was it treatable? Had Grace given up too soon? Was enabling a bad thing if it brought more time to live life and more time for hope? Was addiction Jeremy's moral failure? Did he suffer from some mental disorder? Mandy's epilepsy was deemed neurological and not her fault. Was addiction a disease, possibly genetic, a mental illness, treatable?

I don't know. Is being an enabler all that bad? Is kicking your kid out of the house what a parent should do? Is it ever okay to give up on your child? Would you kick out a kid that had epilepsy, diabetes, or schizophrenia? Is it possible that addiction is a mental disorder? Is there a genetic marker they will find one day? Could it be treated with psychotropic drugs or some kind of medication? Was his addiction something Jeremy could not control? Was his addiction not volitional?

All of these would remain questions to which there were no answers. Grace didn't know, nor did I. But what I did know was that tough love had allowed Jeremy to disappear, to hit rock bottom, and in this case, it meant Jeremy-no-more and never-again.

"You did the best you could," I said to my friend Grace.

"I left him," she said. "I left my baby alone. He was sick. I think I let him die by giving up on him."

And I held my sobbing friend, knowing that what she said was possibly true. That if she had held on to Jeremy, she might still have Jeremy to hold on to.

The Dictator, the Farmer,
and the Professor

The DICTATOR thought
The orange
Was the world
And he squeezed the juice
All over
His hospital robe in the clinic
That bore his name.
"Naughty, naughty," said the nurse
To the man who had ruled a nation.
"Yes, naughty boy," she repeated
As she changed his robe to a fresh one.

———————

The FARMER thought
The orange
Was a seat cushion
And he lifted his crippled body
Laboriously to
Sit on the orange
And the juice got all over his hospital-issued robe.

"Naughty, naughty," said the day nurse.
"Naughty boy," she repeated
And left him dirty
For the night orderly
To change that evening.

————————

The PROFESSOR thought
The orange
Was a book
Peeled it open
To read its contents
Juicing his shirt.
"I'm a naughty boy, Nurse, I'm a naughty boy,"
He said to his wife
And wept at the wet.
She had carefully ironed
And buttoned on his fresh shirt
this once Sunday visit.

————————

And there they were, three men
Divided by continents and duty
United in solidarity
Clearly as homage to the famous
Dr. Alzheimer
Who knew once
How to know an orange
For what it was
And told them
Who they were
Though they would never
Know.

To Sleep or Not to Sleep

THERE ARE two kinds of people in the world—those who can drop off to sleep at the touch of a pillow and those who crush their pillow with tossing and turning. I'm the latter.

As a kid, I remember the annoyance in my mother's voice when I would march into her bedroom at some past-midnight hour announcing tearfully, "Mom, I can't sleep." At which point, she would wearily tell me to count sheep and not to think too much about sleeping. "If you think about sleeping you won't fall asleep," she reminded me.

Really now, how can you not think about sleeping when you're trying to sleep? That's like jumping into a running shower and not getting wet.

I had an emotional problem with the alternative remedy of counting sheep. You see, somewhere around the 155th or 157th jumper, this odd sheep would have an unfortunate and disabling incident. One of his legs would get tangled in the fence and he would "*baah, baah*" relentlessly as if in severe pain. This reoccurring try-to-sleep nightmarish turn of events would keep me up even longer as I tried to coax the lone sheep out of his agonizing entanglement. And it was all my fault. If I hadn't counted him in, he'd probably have been fine.

I also didn't like the word "fall" asleep. My mother tried to convince me that I would "fall" asleep naturally if I stopped trying so hard to "fall" asleep. But I didn't want this fall—like falling down a well or falling into an abyss or falling and hurting myself. Nothing comforting there.

And then my aunt Florence told me if I would just take deep breaths and relax, the sandman would come and visit me. But how could I sleep with the thought of a strange man climbing up the stairs, crawling into my bedroom, and putting sand in my eyes? Who was she kidding? Anyway, Mr. Sandman never came. Gratefully. I guess he couldn't make it up the stairs. We lived in a five-story walk-up.

So from childhood to adulthood and further, I have had a sleep disorder. The world's woes visit me at night and every racing heartbeat I count as my last. Lunesta, Ambien, Benadryl, Sonata, melatonin, Dalmane—these have been my bedtime playmates to no avail. In order to make me drowsy, I have to swallow so many of these pills that I wake up slurring my words and forgetting which planet I have been temporarily assigned to.

And, then, to add to my angst, I read about the punishing, published facts about not getting enough sleep—you eat more if you don't sleep, you shorten your life if you don't sleep, you remember less if you don't sleep, you enjoy sex less if you don't sleep, and you have more accidents with heavy machinery if you don't sleep.

Well, frankly, I don't operate heavy machinery. And this sleepless soul is who I am. Seeking remedies, seeking sleep at any level, I have recently realized that I do some of my best thinking and feeling while tossing and turning. Ideas replace sleep and angst gives momentum to their realization.

I can even write about not sleeping tonight because everyone in my house is sleeping and it's my alone time. The dog is snoring, and I can commune with the stars, a pen, and a pad. So good night, you sleepers. While you play with your subconscious, I'll learn to run on empty while changing the color of my toenail polish from Blushing Red to Party Pink. And I can tell you without a doubt, the new polish will have plenty of nighttime to dry.

The Art of the Faux Pas

*faux pas: This expression originated during the time of Louis XIV. During his reign, dance was so important in the royal courts that to make a false step in any one of the many dances could get you thrown out. It is now a slip or blunder in etiquette, manners, or conduct; an embarrassing social blunder or indiscretion.

**Aphtae epizooticae: Hoof-and-mouth disease; an infectious and sometimes fatal viral disease that affects cloven-hoofed animals, including domestic and wild bovids. Now used colloquially as putting your foot in your mouth.

I AM THE master of the faux pas,* more coarsely known as *Aphtae epizooticae*.** These incidents are part of who I am; I often speak without thinking. My bursts of enthusiasm, I'd like to think, are often innovative and spontaneous ways of looking at a situation. But they seem to come at inappropriate moments.

You see, I have been known to be caught at a dinner party drinking an important guest's water ("Excuse me, Miss, that's my water." "Oh, so sorry, so sorry.") or inappropriately stuffing a stranger's bread roll down while waiting for the first course that never comes soon enough ("Excuse me, Madame, I believe that is my roll." "Oh, so so so sorry."). I once seriously criticized a movie ("It is awful. It is too long. I thought it would never end."), not knowing that the director was sitting next to me. I also once assumed a boss's wife was his daughter. "You're so lovely," I said, "your father must be so proud of you." To which she replied, "He is my husband."

What is this speaking my mind? Where did it come from? It is uncontrollable and often gets me into trouble. And yet it allows me to react honestly and edit films with my gut, which serves the end product. If you think too hard and worry about correctness, you often lose initial instincts that are attributes in a critical game.

The most prominent *faux pas de moi* occurred over the freshly painted portrait of a dear friend. Let's call her Penelope Hightower.

One evening, she invited me over for an elegant soirée at her penthouse to meet her new lothario, Henry Grierson. He was the first non-button-down Wall Street tycoon Penny had ever dated, and she claimed that this Henry, a burgeoning artist, was to be the love of her life.

As I entered her parentally endowed Park Avenue lodging with its original chandeliers and working fireplaces, I noticed a grotesque and somewhat interpretive portrait of my dear friend over the entrance mantelpiece. At the time, Penelope's entrance hallway was the size of most of our shared apartments. After all, it was the 1970s, we were poor, and a studio apartment divided by four inmates made living in New York a possibility.

I expressed with disdain, "This painting of you is atrocious, Penny. You look like Lady Godiva on acid. Your bare tits are not even matched. Jesus, Penny, take it down!"

From her cavernous living room came a sarcastic booming basso voice with a New York lilt. "Ah, you must be Sheila. Glad you like my painting of Penelope. Can you imagine she sat for more than sixteen hours—broken up by a little extra lovin'?" (Despicable, this Henry.) With a deep breath, I introduced myself to him. "Sorry, I have no taste." (I have superb taste.) He smiled arrogantly and insisted his painting was "historical-interpretive, with past and present Penelope once removed from reality intermixed with the truth imbued by the abstract." (Indeed!) I told him I knew very little about art and had been an English major.

Was it a faux pas, or an *Aphtae epizooticae*, or was I a fortune-teller? For though Henry married Penny, taking her last name as his hyphenated name, *Henry Hightower-Grierson*—this marriage would not last. Some twenty years later, I am happy to report Penny's portrait and Henry are long gone. Penelope is re-married to a respectable banker and as far as I know has inherited her family's sizable fortune. Her ex, Henry, having never worked at anything but his failing art career, received a large settlement after a long lawsuit over the Hightower-Grierson family fortune. He made a fool of himself defending himself, suing the estate, and just to silence him, was given a large chunk of change. Their joint child, Athena Aphrodite, is a delightful, brilliant student with no artistic ambition. She's studying to be a brain surgeon. Clearly, Henry's art was a recessive gene; my out-spokenness a dominant one.

So there is good and bad at impetuous commentary. I have tried to learn first reactions can often be between yourself and yourself. For example, *What a piece of shit this film is*, silently. Out loud, "What a great film." Or, silently, *How could you have married such a schmuck?* while out loud, "Good choice. I think he's a very nice guy." But though I try, I am still instinctive, im-petuous, usually right but often wrong. What is it that they say about a zebra and her stripes?

Eavesdropping on Adultery

THE AMTRAK from New York to Providence was much easier than taking a puddle-jumper flight. The seats were comfortable, and I decided to read John Updike's *Endpoint*. This one trip doing something not related to work—just this one time.

I found myself sitting opposite two reasonably attractive women, somewhere in their late forties. They were engaged in a delicious conversation about adultery—and I was transfixed. I did my "pretend-read" act, displaying a deep interest in my book, intently turning the pages that could just as well have been blank.

WOMAN ONE: Yes . . . but frankly it wouldn't matter to me if Chuck screwed around. We've been married nearly thirty years and, let's face it, sex is dull. I fake everything and it's really not that frequent.

WOMAN TWO: How frequent?

WOMAN ONE: The truth?

WOMAN TWO: Of course, Madam Genevieve.

GENEVIEVE: Maybe once a month. Maybe once in two months. Sometimes longer. Who keeps track, Margaret? We're stuck with each other. Isn't that what one calls "mature love"?

MARGARET: They say the pheromones wear off and attraction goes out the window.

GENEVIEVE: What's a phen-a-rome?

MARGARET: A pher-o-mone. It's a smell—one that attracts the sexes, like beetles and apes and a man and a woman. It makes them lusty—for a while, at least.

GENEVIEVE: Well, we ain't got none, ole Chucky and I. We've been with each other since high school. Then it was hot and heavy and panting. Then Chuck had hair. And what about you, Ms. Margaret? Ms. Sexual Silencio?

MARGARET: Boris is just Boris boring.

GENEVIEVE: What does that mean?

MARGARET: Sex was never the mainstay. He's a genius, you know. They won't part with him at Yale. They even matched the Stanford offer.

GENEVIEVE: Boris is certainly smart. No doubt about it. Would you care if he "strayed"?

MARGARET: Boris isn't the straying type.

GENEVIEVE: Why do you say that?

MARGARET: He's like a lab rat. He never leaves his research lab.

GENEVIEVE: I guess like Chuck's addiction to the Red Sox.

MARGARET: At least they're seasonal. Labs are forever— twenty-four seven. They never close. Boris and I have been married for twenty-seven years in February. Oops. No, no, twenty-eight years.

GENEVIEVE: Just like me and Chuck. Chuck is sweet, you could say. I love him in my own way . . . Margaret, I'm exhausted. Shopping wears me out. Want a coffee? It's just two cars up.

MARGARET: Yes, yes, coffee.

GENEVIEVE: With what inside?

MARGARET: This time with heavy cream and Sweet'N Low. I'm a study in contradictions.

After taking a bill out of her wallet, Genevieve got up and moved, swaying with the train. She disappeared as the electric train door let her pass through. It closed. Margaret took her compact and lipstick out of her bag and powdered her nose, then rubbed a bright red lipstick over her lips several times—puckering at her reflection. She suddenly reached for her cell phone and dialed. She checked her face in her compact mirror and watched herself as she talked.

MARGARET (whispering into the phone): Chuck. Hi, my darling. Yes, I'm with her. I am here with Genevieve on Amtrak. We shopped till we dropped. She just went for coffee. Chuck, she has no idea. You would not believe our conversation. She said you have sex. (Pause.) You don't, do you? (Pause.) Yes, I knew it wasn't true. Darling, poopsie, I miss you. I get all gooey just thinking about you. Tomorrow at seven, yes. I want you badly. (Pause.) Me too. I love you too. Got to go, got to go. She's coming back. Adieu, hot pants chili pepper.

Not a moment too soon, Genevieve returned with two cups of coffee tipping to the train's jolts. Margaret put away her mirror and phone.

GENEVIEVE: Darn, guess what? I remembered the cream but forgot your Sweet'N Low. Sorry, sorry. I'll go back.

MARGARET: No difference, I can drink it without it. I'm desperate for caffeine. I love the black blouse you bought. A bit pricey but awfully pretty. Chuck will love you in it.

GENEVIEVE (smiling): Chuck won't even notice, Margaret. Trust me.

MARGARET: I trust you.

And they sipped their coffee staring out the window. The conductor bellowed, "Next stop, New Haven! New Haven, next stop!" The women gathered their packages and waited for the train to come to a halt. And me? I wished John Updike was around to hear them.

Par for the Course

YOUNG MARY #1 was the first cousin of the president's wife. The president successfully ran IDCo, the Incredible Digital Company. Mary #1 was related by birth to the president's second cousin's aunt—a troubling but overlooked genetic connection—as her aunt was also the niece of the father of the president's brother. So no one was surprised when Mary #1 got a summer internship at IDCo. And guess what, without an interview. Correction: the interview would take place after this well-connected Mary #1 had gotten the job. She did fill out an application, but by then she was ensconced at her desk at her new job. The story of her accomplishment was told at the seventh hole by the president's wife, who bragged that her brilliant cousin, Mary #1, had completed all the interviews and passed with flying colors. The entire family were great golfers and always shot par, with Mary #1 being first in the junior league at the Piney Ridge Golf Course.

The other Mary, let's call her Mary #2, had no connections. Her application had been selected from a lottery of applicants from ten colleges and she was the lucky winner. Her father was a postman who had been bitten by a dog. Mary #2's mother, the nurse, wanted him to get rabies shots, but Mary #2's father refused. Passing it off as a wee nip, he would die ten days later of rabies. "Don't bother, don't bother. It barely broke my skin," he had said. So be it. Sad, but true. Mary #2 and her mother and her brother would trudge on. Her mom continued her nursing career but used caution when dealing with male bravado and men who claimed there was nothing wrong with them. Mary #2's brother could no longer afford college. He got a job installing new cable connections for customers who were always complaining about reception.

And so it would come to pass that both Marys, though unknown to each other, landed summer jobs working in similar areas at IDCo. They may have nodded in the cafeteria, as one does to strangers, but they were never actually aware of each other's presence. One day Mary #1 even received an e-mail by mistake for Mary #2. She would inquire as to another Mary and then pass it along correctly. But that was the extent of their communication.

In their last year of college, Mary #1 graduating from a tony girl's school and Mary #2 from a fine city college, both would look for their first full-time positions. They had received similar write-ups from Human Resources for their performances during their summer jobs, and both looked forward to starting their careers at companies as prestigious IDCo.

Now Mary #1, who was the first cousin of the president's wife, related also by birth to the president's second cousin's aunt, who was the niece of the father of the president's brother (who was also, by the way, the godfather of the cousin's adopted brother, whose ex-wife used to play golf with the president's mother, whose brother had a favorite partner, who was Mary's father), would be offered her job immediately upon graduation. With an application included in the acceptance letter. How odd indeed. Mary #1 rushed to the Piney Ridge Golf Course, where her father was at the watering hole, to deliver the news.

Mary #1's father said, "Congratulations, Mary! You did it! You did it!" and Mary beamed, for she felt her worth as both a champion golfer and an applauded job seeker.

Mary #2 would have to laboriously fill out a five-page application to IDCo, which asked her to cite the splendor of the company, why she was the right person for the job, and how she would expand the company's goals into the future.

She waited anxiously to hear from IDCo. After several weeks, Mary #2 received a reply. She opened it nervously.

> *Dear Mary #2,*
>
> *We so appreciate your requesting a job at IDCo after your excellent achievement as a summer intern. We have reviewed your application and in the area where you applied, there are regretfully no vacancies.*
>
> *We will keep you in mind when the next opening occurs. We wish you luck with your job search.*
>
> > *Regards,*
> > *The IDCo team*

And so it would be that Mary #1 had gotten her first job and Mary #2 would have to keep looking and looking—getting a temporary job, ironically, in the gift shop at the Piney Ridge Golf Course.

And then one Sunday after her first successful week at work, Mary #1 would be playing golf with her father and realize she had forgotten her sun visor.

"Darn, Dad," she said to her father. "I left my visor at home." She then hopped in a cart and was driven by a downtrodden caddy to the gift shop and unbeknownst to her, and neither Mary knowing the connection, would ask Mary #2 for a visor.

"Charge it to my father," said Mary #1, "Henry Smith III" (who was the favorite partner of the brother whose ex-wife used to play golf with the president's mother and who was the niece of the father of the president's brother blah blah blah and also the godfather of the cousin's adopted brother, related by birth to the president's second cousin's aunt, and was also the father of Mary #1, the cousin of president's wife). Phew.

Mary #2 then replied, "Sure," while handing Mary #1 the visor, which cost as much as Mary #2's daily pay before taxes from the Piney Ridge Golf Course. "Have a good game," said Mary #2.

"Thanks," said Mary #1 politely, before dashing back to play.

As was par for the course. For life would continue for both Marys, as the seesaw they were on would never be even.

And that was how the game was played on the course.

And that was how the game would be played in life, though Mary #2 was determined to make herself an exception to the rules of the game.

Trudie Foodie

THIS IS Trudie Foodie's diet wish list:

- She wants to not think of food most of the time.
- She wants to say, "No dessert please."
- She wants to hate butter on her bread.
- She wants to believe pasta is her enemy.
- She wants to like going to bed hungry.
- She wants to not lick freshly made chocolate pudding from the pan.
- She wants to go down four sizes.
- She never wants to see XL on the back of a pair of pants.
- She wants to wear her blouses tucked in.
- She wants the refrigerator to not be a destination spot.
- She wants to not daydream about what's in the minibar before she enters the hotel room.
- She wants to learn to throw away leftovers.
- She wants to say, "This is too sweet."
- She wants to drink her coffee black, without heavy cream.
- She wants people to think she's too skinny.
- She wants to not fixate on a doughnut, or an éclair, or a sundae.

- She wants to be in control of her next bite instead of being bitten by desire.
- She wants to be loved as a Rubens, not aspire to be a Modigliani.
- She wants to move to a country where women can be as fat as men—where ageism and weightism do not rule.

So who is Trudie Foodie? Well, Trudie is the kind of person who rarely asks for help. She is insistent about putting her own luggage, however heavy, on the airplane overhead rack. Therefore, it is odd and slightly out of character for her to admit the above. But, quite simply, she cannot seem to diet successfully. She can lick almost any dragon but cannot put this fire out.

Trudie is not obese and is relatively well preserved for her impatient advancing years (or so she likes to think—who wouldn't?) and yet, she must confess that she is clearly overweight. The bathroom mirrors, catching her naked self, do not lie. No sooner does she leave the tub then she quickly wraps herself in a large bath towel. Can you imagine being fearful and dismayed by your own reflection? When she shops, she looks for camouflage, not clothes.

Trudie is not asking for skinny—though she did grow up to the constant refrain: "How do you eat so much?" meaning, "You eat so much, how do you stay so thin?" No more. Her all-grown-up size does not elicit such comments. The best she can hope for is, "You're not fat really," and frankly this is simply a lie. She is fat. F-A-T.

She wishes she could adjust to her newfound postmenopausal mean-spirited plumpness. But she can't. You see to her, fat is a sign of defeat. An admission of acceptance of less than her very best. A profound recognition of being out of control. The fact, simply emerging, that she is a victim of her own victimization. That she is lazy and slothful. That this lardiness is not under her control. As a control freak, to Trudie Foodie these notions are unacceptable, intolerable. "Me? Can't be me," she says to herself. And yet, by God, it is her very self.

You see, one cookie is not enough. Ice cream must have whipped cream. And when she returns home, she asks herself, "Now, where did I put the fudge?" She can send to the diner for apple-crumb cake and then obsess on the length of delivery time. *Did they hear me? Should I call again? Should I cancel my order?* No. Absolutely not. Never cancel food. Pointless. Her ancestors were starving people.

What is this urge to fill the vacuum that is already full? Did she need an analyst? Or was it too late? Why do some people leave edible food on their plates? Why do skinny girls fill up so quickly? Trudie wondered. Why does she go on automatic pilot when food—McDonald's or pheasant—is put in front of her? She does not discriminate. To be served is to eat. To eat is to complete.

Was there a movie Trudie Foodie could go to without a large-size Raisinets or Kit Kat to devour? Was there popcorn without butter? Was there a birthday without that extra piece of cake? "Oh, I shouldn't . . ." but she would. Is there a moment that couldn't be filled with a Dunkin' donut hole—and then another?

Should Trudie succumb to this size fourteen or struggle to regain her lost size eight mothy jeans waiting patiently for the good ole days, while gathering mildew in her closet? Let's face it, she could barely pull these pants over her monstrous middle.

Should Trudie Foodie just toss this "weightfulness" to the wind, so little time to partake of pleasure, so few sweets in life left, and just adjust to her plentitude and eat on? Or should she try to control her desires and close her mouth to mastication and continue to pursue the impossible dream of loss—a leaner, smaller self?

Trudie saw herself as the personification of a gluttonous Thanksgiving—stuffing down her own stuffing. She was carrying a twenty-five-pound turkey under her smock top. *I am the gift of Christmas Past and Christmas Present. I am the gift of Christmas Future who keeps on eating,* she thought. *Bah humbug. Come New Year's Eve, I'll resolve to diet. Come New Year's Day— I'll compulsively eat everything in sight. And soon I'll be unbuttoning my pants and loosening my bra, and not for any romantic adventure—alas. Oh, and by the way, did anyone see where I put the seven-layer cake? I can smell it, I can almost taste it. I must have it.*

Poor Trudie.

Her Disappearing Act

HE SAID she was plumpish, her husband, again, and again, and again. How could he love someone so plumpish? And it was true. She was fattish. Wooed by the lure of a potato chip. The silky softness of ice cream—rocky road. The beauty of a buttered croissant—hot, of course.

You see, once she had been thin. Even skinny. She had been blessed with a fast metabolism. But then one day her luck ran out and her metabolism died in the middle of a hot fudge sundae. And so to get her thin, loved self back, and to show her husband she could, she decided to eat—nothing. Sometimes a pea. Green. Or a bean. Lima. Or a tiny sip of water.

And so weeks passed. She got smaller and smaller and smaller. Until one day she disappeared completely in front of his very eyes. He could no longer see her. And though she was invisible to him, she was happy with her new self—free from his critical eye. But he, her husband, was unquestionably lonely without his plumpish wife.

Mammogram Day

WE SIT in pink robes with smiley faces on them. My robe has no ties. I say to a lady more elderly than I . . . "My robe has no ties."

"You have it on inside out," she says. We giggle quietly.

"Oh," I say. "I'll just clutch it." Cold hands. A dear-life clutch. This is probably my thirtieth mammo and it never gets easier. Scarier as more friends succumb. Although Annie's wig is a good one, I shudder. My hair is my best feature. Wigs are hot. Wigs are itchy.

Why me? I think. Then, *Why not me?*

The why-not-me prophecy gets worse with each passing year. So far I have escaped being caught. I hate this waiting room—the old magazines, the older women—some better preserved than others. Yet their flesh-and-blood faces are pale. Eyes catching, occasionally we exchange knowing fake smiles. Birds of a feather with no place to fly. The room has no windows. I guess it's better this way. No place to jump. It's cold under this pink-flimsy. A frail woman asks for a blanket. She shivers. The blanket she gets looks like army surplus. Now I'm alone on the Island of Mammo in an air-raid shelter. Silent sirens sound imminent attack. Next to me, a loosely tied pink gown opens and a younger woman quickly covers a scarred, breastless chest. She stares at me, she knows what I saw. No pretenses in pink gowns.

"I have BRCA2."

"Oh," I say. "Will you be okay?"

"My sister died of it at forty, but my eighty-year-old mother is still alive and she had it."

"You'll be all right," I say. "You look terrific." We gray smile. She knows I know nothing. My heart pounds. Or is it hers?

They call my name. I enter the chamber and my breasts are squeezed into mammogram silence. The technician indicates nothing. I want her to like me. If I'm nice to her, maybe I can influence the results. *"Too nice for cancer,"* she'll say. *"I'll let her go."* I cajole her into a terse relationship.

"Once I had an A cup. Now I'm a C," I say in an offhanded manner.

"It happens," she says, revealing nothing. She has been trained by science to keep deadly secrets. Top clearance.

Back in the waiting room, I remember Eddie at fourteen and the first tit-squeeze. It was fun, but not worth this waiting room. No tit-ulation here. No lovers, however hot and handy, could pay the price of panic in this Madison Avenue Hellhole. I have been here for two hours. Pretending to read *Vogue*. An article on foot padding for flat feet. The same paragraph read again and again. New injectables can make over feet so anyone can wear stilettos. I'll get this padding if I live . . .

Please, Ms. Wintour, I promise, just get me out of here. Anna, are you ever scared, or are you so insulated you breeze through this agony of discovery? Now you see it. Now you don't. Now you see it. Where do you go, Anna? Probably mammos on the beach in Belize. Sequined smiley faces on designer gowns, I bet.

Oh God, get me outta here. Dr. Mephisto is probably studying my X-ray and counting the few days I have left on Earth. She doesn't have the heart to tell me. That's why the wait is so long. She's never seen anything so horrible before.

Suddenly, they call my name. They congratulate me on my free and clear breasts. Dr. Mephisto shows me two breasts on a screen. I guess they're mine. Dr. Mephisto says everything looks fine. I love this woman. I must rename her. I will see her again next year.

I pay four hundred dollars for this fun-house ride and make an appointment. Same time, same place, same breasts, I hope. But I'm sick of them really. Bosom buddies who can turn on you ain't no friends at all.

Labor Day Weekend Labors:
A Hateful Three Days

S O, YOU want to know about my Labor Day Weekend?

Awful awfulness.

So here it goes.

The weather was perfect, which I despise. Waiting for my guests, there was no excuse on this perfect day to see a rainy-day shitty movie at the six-plex and laugh myself silly. No excuse to shop and buy something not needed, wear it once, and then regret buying it. Stuck in a perfect day.

Then they arrived. My son, his current girlfriend—blond and beautiful, smart and sweet, the perfect mother for my imagined future grandchildren. And with her—her mother, Madame Suzanne Daumier—the inspector general. I threw out my arms and said, "Welcome, Suzy," to which she replied, "Call me Suzanne." I'd never met this mother before. She claimed to be an esteemed teacher of romance languages. Unfortunately, her plane was on time. Holiday planes are not supposed to be on time.

I could tell from the moment she looked at me that we were not going to be friends. I didn't like her. She didn't like me. It was instant. At least we could agree on something. She judged me. She said she'd die for my thick curly black hair. It's brown really. She didn't die. She lived for three days and three nights.

These are some of the lowlights.

Friday evening:

Early to bed, a saccharine good night to Madame—the lovebirds had already retired. They would be gone for the weekend and off on their own. It was ordained, therefore, that I was to be the sole caretaker of this bitch—my husband married to tennis, my son and his girlfriend—well, you know.

Day 1: Saturday lowlights

Awoke at 6 a.m. for some alone time. Alas, not to be. Madame had had trouble sleeping, and so there she was so bright and early—in the kitchen, and stretched out on the floor. Palms up. Yup. She explained she felt this hard-floor posture was important as it helped align her chakras. Excusing myself for stepping over her, I explained I was longing for coffee. Caffeine was not her thing, she said, shuddering at the thought. She had brought her own fresh mint from—you guessed it—she was from Southern California.

I suggested calmly that we microwave some of her special tea. She informed me that microwaving was dangerous and that she preferred her tea at a slow, slow, natural boil. Sipping my radio-waved coffee, I carefully prepared her specialty tea. She said that she could hear from the sound of the heated bubbling water that it was teatime. This Alice from her own Wonderland never left the floor. Lying-down tea was required. I stepped over her to get her a cup and bent all the way down to serve her. She drank the tea slowly while stretched out flat. Don't ask me how.

I gulped my coffee stiffly erect while chatting downward. Soon, too soon, she would rise up from the floor, but not until she ohmmed some ohms and repeated some mantra. I thought to myself, *Oh, Buddha save me!*

I drank several strong cups of poisoned coffee. I needed extra alertness. What followed would be an excruciating day of small talk.

For example:
> SHE: Didn't your face-lift doctor jump out the window?
> ME: No.
> SHE: Oh.
> ME: What gave you that idea?
> SHE: I thought it was common knowledge.
> ME: No.
> SHE: Maybe it was his wife who jumped.
> ME: No, not true . . . his personal life is his own anyway.
>   Shall we move on?
> SHE: Well, your face, it seems he did a very good job; you
>   can *hardly* tell.
> ME: Have you read any good books lately?

Who says time goes faster as you age? I thought a day had only twenty-four hours. Not on this Labor Day Weekend it didn't. My poor little boy, my little boy-beautiful-blue, was in love with the wrong mother's daughter. The mother was dragging her fucking umbilical cord all over my spotless country house. This clawing *Madame Suzanne*, with her mid-Atlantic accent, talked of her lovers (she was divorced thrice) and her reincarnation from an evil muskrat from which she was learning life lessons. She spoke of her guru, her past lives, her salvation by yoga, her constipation tea, her new spiritual awakening, and her near-death experience—close, but not close enough. There was no bright light at the end of this tunnel.

Day 2: Sunday lowlights

Madame lay by the pool.

A slinky robe covered her soon-to-be-discovered self.

The gardener's son, Mackie, a handsome, shy twenty-year-old, was clearly the object of her inappropriate desire.

She stripped off her robe seductively and underneath was a too-small bikini, probably too-too tight for even an anorexic model.

Madame's bulges and belly button burst over her skimpy bottom.

She spoke flirtatiously to Mackie, saying, "Beautiful boy, with those beautiful hands—I can see why you make plants grow."

Poor young Mackie. He smiled helplessly while trying to prune a fading bush.

And then came the pièce de résistance.

Bending over my pool with her voluminous breasts peeking, she sniffed the water. My pool water. My expensive water—this chlorinated bromide pool was hard-earned by me.

"Chemicals," she said with distain. "I only swim in salt water."

Taking her quart bottle of Evian (mine), she doused her plenitude. "Evaporation is from the gods," she said. What was she talking about?

She poured more Evian over herself.

Wanting to kill her, I exclaimed I was hot and going inside.

"Mack," I said to the young man, frozen in the heat of the day, "Come with me, dear. I want you to look at a dying petunia."

The traumatized boy gladly followed. And so it would come to pass that Mackie and I barely survived Day 2.

Day 3: Monday lowlights

Almost over.

A farewell lunch at the local grill.

She asked the waitress to swear the olive oil was extra virgin and from Italy.

She also inquired and asked for information about her vegetarian omelet. Was the egg-laying chicken free range and were the vegetables farm-to-table and organic as well?

The poor waitress.

She then displayed some thirty pills tightly packed in a cellophane baggie. She assured me these daily supplements were specially prepared by the best doctor in L.A. Each pill was engaged in preserving one of her chubby organs—one for her liver, one for her pancreas, one to keep her kidneys from getting stones, etc., etc., and a rather large capsule for sexual enhancement. "Hard to swallow this pill," she said, "but it works," winking at me.

My tip was over-the-top generous. Earned.

The time for her departure was not a moment too soon.

Madame was picked up by a limo and rushed to the airport at my expense. She dared not be late. She dared not pay for anything. I warned her about holiday planes, you know. Let's hurry. We hugged a phony good-bye. Good-bye my dear Suzanne Daumier.

I tipped the sensitive limo driver twenty dollars extra for being early. I know he felt my pain.

I've just had a bagel with full-fat cream cheese, a big cup of microwaved coffee with whole cream and some real sugar. I've earned all those extra calories. I took my one silver Centrum multivitamin and swam ferociously in my polluted pool. *I'll be damned*, I thought.

I returned to New York driving too fast and crawled into bed under my favorite down quilt. Hot, yes, but comforting. Baby warm. Alone. Husband, son, and possible future daughter-in-law were to stay on in the country for a few days.

Later that evening, Madame's daughter called, telling me that her mother had landed. The possible grandmother of my future grandchildren was unfortunately safe and grounded.

This Madame Suzanne Daumier must never return. Of this I was sure.

And the weather is still perfect. But most importantly . . .
   I had lived through this laborious Labor Day Weekend.

A Dog's Dying

TODAY OUR dog, Cornwallis, received a death sentence.

I thought he just had some tick disease so I went to the gym. When I came back, I learned by telephone that he had a few weeks to live. The vet said his platelets were five hundred times below normal. It was leukemia—lymphoma, blastoma, gastlioma, whatever—and there was no cure. All we could do was keep him out of pain.

This son of a bitch was the mutt of my dreams. Cornwallis is a dog, not a human being. I know that, and yet my human heart is broken. So is my son's. So is my husband's. He's family. My eyes are swollen, my lips are puffy. I want to hold him and give him some of my own time that's left. That crazy barter is just how much I love him. His liver and his spleen are swollen. They will return my wounded lover tomorrow and I will watch him grow weak and die.

Let me tell you about Corny. Corny has seen me through some rough times. He knows my secrets, even the ones I don't tell him. I know this through his eyes. He is a male dog but he was my best girlfriend. To my family's dismay I always referred to him as "her." He was my girl, and when my girlfriend (the human one), my college roommate, tragically died, Corny consoled me like no one else. Corny was afraid of thunder and lightning—mortified. When he would tremble, I would whisper into his ears my fears, making him feel he and I were one. I even gave him a bite of my Ativan (a benzo tranquilizer) mixed with some peanut butter and jelly. This concoction was our special scary-day secret. During the worst lightning strike, we held each other close for comfort. We were anxiety sweethearts.

I'm telling you all this because I want to share this love in case one day, somewhere, he gets a chance to read about him and me. I want him to know how much I admire his valor, his protection, and his proud muttiness. With a thoroughbred heart, Corny never forgot he was a rescue dog from a Bronx tenement. His nose was never in the air. He sniffed out earthly dangers and never let go of his street smarts. He traveled from Park Avenue to Litchfield County, ate quality pet food, had fancy pet collars and leashes, but he was never smug. Wet nose down. Tail up. Nothing made my girl happier than rolling in muddy green grass, defying his expensive recent shampoo. No bear, no deer, no snake, no rabbit, no frog could outsmart him. He knew his place in the scheme of living things. Even Darwin would have recognized his reaching up and out—his superior self. Corny had a ferocious bark. He would warn us equally of approaching friend or foe, but he also had a purr sound he must have stolen from a stray cat.

So Corny, I promise you, I will not let you suffer. I will not prolong your cancer agony. I will go with you and take control of your destiny, and when you die, you'll die with dignity in my arms. I love you fiercely, and I thank you for being my friend (I know I'm not easy). You have forever changed the oldest of expressions, for it is no longer a man's but a woman's best friend.

My Cornwallis.

First Kiss

She ran into her early love on the streets of
N.Y.C.
Sweet love from decades ago,
Fifty years.
He was elderly now.
"Judith," he said,
"Oh my God."
He was her very first tongue kiss.
Her rubber-band braces snapped
And almost blinded him
During spin-the-bottle in
Elaine Zeckendorf's mothy closet.
(Does anyone use mothballs anymore?)
Memory so clear,
Fifty years ago,
A moment.
And there he was
Fifty years in snap crackle,
And here he was
And they exchanged
Niceties.
Doctor lawyer Indian chief
Rich man poor man beggar man thief

Solomon Grundy born on Monday
Wednesday's child is full of woe
And then gone
Down the cement block.
She turned back to catch a glimpse of then,
He was gone.
Her heart pounding hard,
A blueprint,
And she knew
She had been there,
Young.

I Hated Teddy and
Teddy Hated Me

I hated Teddy and Teddy hated me.
The problem was he was the dearest buddy of
my son.
Teddy was a hamster.
David, my son, was human. (Well, most of the time.)

It started like this.

David had no siblings.
He had a dog, Hammy, whom he loved.
But at five, he assumed all four-legged animals were
for riding.
And so we often had to save Hamburger (his full
name) *from David yelling, "Giddy up, giddy up,*
Hammy!"
I would dash in to remove this child who saw his
beloved dog as a bucking bronco.

But Hammy was all-forgiving and adored David, whatever the price.

We reasoned, "David, be gentle. You weigh forty-five pounds, he weighs thirty. Please do not ride him."

And so at least when we saved Hammy by these numbers, his racetrack days were over.

All was at peace with this beloved canine.

———————

The bone of contention still was Teddy.

Teddy was not just a hamster in a cage.

Teddy was from the Upper East Side of Manhattan. He was a rodent's rodent with claws and a spiteful little bite.

So when I suggested to the salesman at the pet store we would need a cage, he looked aghast and said,

"We don't do cages. We do habitats."

"Of course," I said.

David had riffled through a bunch of rodent-looking hamsters, picking one, then another, and eventually picking what seemed to be the largest and meanest of the litter.

He named him Teddy.

And some three hundred dollars later, Teddy was outfitted with tubes and byways, highways and turnarounds, all leading to a Ferris wheel that said TED (three letters were free). Teddy even had a cotton-padded bed.

———————

David was beside himself with joy.

I was not.

Carrying a rattling cage, I mean habitat, Ferris wheel, and what looked like a hamster's double bed, we *arrived home to great approval from the doorman, who was especially entranced by the bed.*

I told him there was no chance in the world Teddy would be having company.

David carried Teddy separately in a Chinese food carton.

He spoke softly to him. "I love you, Teddy."

Within hours of setting up Teddy's duplex apartment, this hamster began to rule our house.

Back from a sleepover, David would burst through the door as I waited for a "Missed you, Mom! Missed you!"

Asking only, "How's Teddy?"

"Fine, fine," I replied, with Hammy panting. He clearly felt rejected too.

———————

For hours my very bright son would play with this miniature beast. Much to my dismay, they would scamper through the house with me eeking, "Put that thing away. I'm serious, put it away."

"You hate Teddy."

"No, I don't."

"Yes, you do."

"No, I don't!"

Well, I did.

Sometimes I felt like Snow White's stepmother.

I would come home to a dark house, thinking evil thoughts.

David would be sound asleep and I would menacingly glance at Teddy.

He would be playing dead inside one of his habitat's tubes.

I thought maybe his time had finally come.

*After all, I had looked up his life expectancy—two
years.*
We were going on three.
And then, as if he read my mind,
Teddy would wink and rush to his Ferris wheel,
Take a few twirls and roll up in his bed.
He never failed to perform after lifting my hopes up.

———————

More than his presence, I hated his smell.
His cage required cleaning.
Unlike Hammy, Teddy shit where he ate.
And I'm not sure he knew the difference.
*I hated his supercilious attitude and David's passionate
attachment to this creature.*

———————

*One summer David went away for one week to a
sleepaway camp.*
*My devoted husband, Sidney, who had taken a fancy
to Teddy,*
Asked me to help clean the exclusive habitat.
*This had been a father-son bonding experience, I was
happy to say,*
But now with David away, it was my duty.

———————

*To do so, Teddy had to be lifted up and new, clean
stuffing laid.*
*I helped begrudgingly as Sid lifted and cleaned the
cage with veterinarian-approved disinfectant so as not to
harm Teddy's respiratory system.*

During this procedure, I held Teddy by his tail.

"Hurry!" I said to Sidney. "Clean it faster! I'm going to puke!"

Sidney took the garbage into the other room to toss.

I held Teddy up by his hideous tail.

He was having a fun time swinging and doing rodent calisthenics. And then after a major swing, daring not to look and with my eyes tightly shut, I heard a thud.

Teddy had fallen into the empty cage before Sid had returned to replenish it with fresh cotton. Teddy fell from my grip, scampering carefree.

He was fine, it appeared, racing to his Ferris wheel for a spin. I, sadly and sickly, was left holding his tail.

I had dismembered Teddy.

His tail was in my hand and he was scampering in the cage seemingly unharmed.

———————

I screamed to Sidney who was dumping out the cage shavings in the other room.

"Sid!" I cried. "I pulled off his tail!"

He rushed in. "What did you do?"

"I didn't. Teddy did."

"You did what?"

"He swung off his tail. Look!" I dropped the tail in the cage.

"He might eat it!" Sidney said. My husband was very logical. "You should wrap it up and we'll call the vet. Maybe they can reattach it."

"Can't he live without a tail?" I asked, hoping not.

"Why should he?" my husband responded. "He came with a tail." My husband had clearly lost any respect for me. We rushed to the phone.

The vet, Dr. Pigman, was rescuing a dog that had swallowed a marble. She finally picked up.

And then Sid said, as men will do, that his wife had held Teddy by the tail and that Teddy had fallen off his tail.

Sweet Dr. Pigman assured us that hamsters can live without a tail, but cleanliness was the goal.

We would have to keep his anal cavity bacteria-free to prevent infection from his feces.

I had to lie down and cover my face.

Sidney consoled me, saying, "Dr. Pigman said we could bring Teddy in for a visit to see if there was any anal tearing. But if we kept the area clean, the hamster would be fine, even with a little tear."

Daily Neosporin would keep Teddy from getting any infection.

I panicked.

Teddy would live, and I was clearly his nurse.

After all, as my husband kept repeating, if I had held him in my arms instead of being revolted and holding him by his tail, this dismemberment would never have happened.

———

And so it came to pass that, every night for that long week, I would come home from work and Q-tip Teddy's arse.

A reason to never come home again, for no soap was strong enough to wipe away this hateful cleansing.

But we did it. My husband with humor, and me with abiding disgust.

———

Alas, the day came when David returned from camp.

Dropping his trunk at the door, he rushed in to see his beloved hamster.

At first, all was fine.

Teddy scampered, he was fed, David seemed not to notice, saying, "Hi, Teddy! I'm home!"

When suddenly some hours later we heard a scream from his room.

"Teddy has no tail!"

"Yup," said Sidney. "Mom held him by the tail when I was cleaning the cage. Dr. Pigman says he doesn't need a tail if we keep him clean."

"Mom what?!" David exclaimed.

"Mom held him by the tail and he fell," Sidney explained.

"Mom what?!" David cried.

"She didn't mean it."

"Oh, yes, she did! She hates Teddy!"

"I do not," I interjected.

"You do too," David replied.

"Okay, I'm not crazy about him, but I would never do anything like that deliberately," I conceded.

"Yes, you would."

"No, I wouldn't. Stop it, David—he's just a hamster and he's fine."

"He has no tail!"

"I know he has no tail but he will live and he will be fine."

"You tried to kill Teddy!"

"I did not! Don't be a child."

"I am a child."

"I'll buy you another hamster. I am really sorry."

"You are not."

"Yes, I am. Now stop it."

He flung himself tragically on his bed. I held my sobbing little boy and promised him the moon, but all he wanted was Teddy's tail back.

"We can't do that," I said.

And so it came to pass that Teddy got himself a friend, another male hamster with a tail,

And David sort of forgave me and quit blaming his hardworking, hamster-hating mom as Teddy was no longer lonely, which seemed like some form of compensation.

———————

But that's not the end of Teddy's revenge.

———————

One dismal day, as luck wouldn't have it, I peeked into Teddy's cage, hoping for the best, and Teddy 2 and Tailless Teddy, as he began to be known,

Had a litter. Yes, babies. Not one, not two, but five.

Teddy 2 was clearly not a boy, so Tara, as she began to be known, now had five children.

This family would need a bigger apartment, and so it would be that we would add additional habitats.

I surrendered to these villages, for Teddy had outsmarted me.

Which proves that a rat is a rat is a rat,

And that a working mother can't win.

The Humble Beginnings of My Somewhat Spiritual Self

IT STARTED when I was twelve, with my period. I had an inkling that I was somehow related to the universe because how else would the moon have had a direct line to my ovaries? Every twenty-eight days, like clockwork, with accuracy rivaling Big Ben, these two entities—the moon and my eggs—would be in precise and direct communication. Blood brothers they were. Or was it sister and brother?

Years later, when I tried to explain these celestial occurrences to my college roommate, Stephanie, she said I was turning into a Woodstock "woo-woo" and would soon be running braless on campus. These collegiate put-downs silenced any intimations of immortality for many decades to come. My roommate was a political science major mired in realpolitik.

So I went around for years doing earthly things, gathering and spending and toiling and focusing on rising in the corporate world, giving little attention to the wonder of my chance placement under the magic pull of the stars and the heavens.

But one day, several years ago, I was minding my own business when suddenly a searing sharp pain pierced my right side, forcing me to crawl and scream. On my gurney-foxhole I may even have prayed to God for the pain to stop, though the latter salutation may be revisionist thinking.

Rushed to the ER, child-doctors poked and X-rayed my crumpled self, revealing angry stones lodged in an organ I had never paid any attention to, a tiny, little spiteful thing called a gallbladder that was angrily erupting between my liver and my pancreas.

Two days later, some forty-eight stones were delivered to my hospital bed, where I lay in a stupor. Dr. Morrissey, one of the few remaining "doctors of yore," smiled and held my hand reassuringly and tightly. He said the green vomitus would recede and life without bile would return. He presented me a urine cup with a tight green lid labeled, 48 PRECIOUS STONES: SHEILA NEVINS'S GALLSTONES. Touched by this handwritten cup, yet in a haze, the significance of the gift eluded me.

Some twenty-four hours later, pain and gallbladder were ancient history and I was ready for a pastrami sandwich with hot mustard. I was also primed to appreciate my gift. I opened the urine cup and there they were, glittering pebbles, nature pebbles, outdoor pebbles from inside of me. Forty-eight of them, matching exactly the millions of pebbles placed all over the courtyard of my house in the country. Now I could accept this pebble-match as a mere simple finding. Yet I gasped and cried, and waxing poetic, I sobbed to my husband that I was a spiritual being, part of the universe. "Just look at my stones!" This dearest of men was more than relieved to relinquish me to this newfound universe, having nursed me back to health (I am not a good patient) for an exhausting week.

But yesterday came the spiritual pièce de résistance. Owing to my increasing anxiety and workload and panic over what I believed was an imminent heart stoppage, I agreed to what my kind internist, Dr. Katz, suggested—an echocardiogram. This would be a test to calm my jitters and prove that the end was not near. I did what he said. Staring at the ceiling of the examination room I had suddenly entered my own Sistine Chapel. The stone-faced technician allowed me to listen to the symphony of the chambers of my brave heart. I could hear its heart-wrenching beat.

With false bravado, I asked this conductor for a clue to my terminal diagnosis. "Could I run the marathon?" I asked him.

"With practice," he answered, without giving a glimmer of hope.

But, oh, the sound I heard from my heart—the last supper of my own song—my heart was beautiful. Musical sunshine from quadrant to quadrant, quatrains of whales and oceans and birds and me. A quartet of chambers worthy of a sellout at Lincoln Center.

Assured that my heart was alive and well by my doctor, I breathed easily and returned home that fateful evening to announce to my skeptical family that I had discovered my spiritual self. "I am a whole person," I bellowed dramatically. "I believe that I am part of the natural world from my period, to my gallstones, to my sonorous heartbeat."

Matter-of-factly, my son replied, "Please, Mom, don't get carried away. Can you pass the mashed potatoes?"

And I did.

Picture Perfect
(Almost)

IT WAS a beautiful photograph. She looked stunning. The increasing puffiness under her left eye was gone. The furrowed brow smoothed over. And the fuzzy bangs now silky. Everyone commented on how well she looked in the picture. "You look great in that photograph. Young. Perfect." And it was true.

The problem was, however, it didn't look like her. She was not young and perfect, so sorry to tell. Yet, she liked this likeness of her perfect self. The *Dorian Gray* of her. This once-was-youthful pretty her of her. But she worried about the continual adulation. The picture was perfectly untrue, over the top.

Why did everyone say this picture was so perfect? So youthful? So beautiful? She knew the answer. She dialed. Ringgg, ringgg.

"Edgar," she said to the famous photographer late one night (an adoring friend who never slept and watched old movies). "Sorry to call you so late, Gar Gar, but you know the picture, the one of me that you said was so perfect?"

"Thank you," he said, missing the point.

"Edgar, I want to take the picture again."

"It's beautiful, you liked it," he said. "Shadow and light perfection."

"Yes," she said, "but I don't recognize me."

"It's you," he said. "Silly glamour queen. I saw you there. I took the picture."

"It's a fix," she said. "A gambler's dream. A manipulated fight against time. An assured winner. I want me back in the ring. Or at least try me. Just me. No fix."

And so Edgar reluctantly agreed, in light natural, to ban Photoshopping and to arrange a new shoot. Just a likeness. So, in a flash, the picture would be as she was.

But Edgar still wanted to touch up the upper lip shading, just a drop.

"Smooth the jawline, darling. Just a little, sweetheart."

"Leave it," she said. "Don't fix it, Gar Gar. Send it. Print it. Post it."

"You like it?" he asked quizzically.

"I think so," she said. "I'll get used to it. I'll try the real me on."

Back on the lecture circuit, she went to speak of what she knew. With this new picture—the face she saw in the mirror. Makeup, mascara, rouge, not naked but true to simple paint, as it was, and so it was that she presented herself. The best without appropriated defacing alteration.

A woman came up to her after a talk about a film—a good talk—and said, "You're so much prettier than your picture in the catalogue."

And she said, "Thank you." And smiled to her very core. For she knew her lecture had been a good one and that her animated true self, devoted to her craft, was better than any still touch-up. She glowed with the satisfaction of knowing that it was no crime to be less than perfect.

That night she called dear Edgar. "Gar, dear, I love the picture," she said.

"So be it," he said. "I think you are nuts, but I love you, *darling,* to death. Can we talk in the morning, lovey? I'm watching *Flying Down to Rio*. 1933. Fred Astaire and Ginger Rogers. Divine!"

"Enjoy," she said and put on her night cream, catching a glimpse of an older self in the mirror, to then sleep soundly while dreaming of flying herself.

To Lose a Child

I watched my friend suffer
When her child died.
And I knew that she would die
Though breathing
For the rest of her life.

———————

Your child's pain is greater
Than your pain.
The agony of birthing repeated
With the slightest wound
To this soul of your soul.

———————

Baby has a fever.
Mommy's heart stops.
But death
Is unspeakable heat
Burning fire forever
Never to be put out.

My friend is lost to this world.
She has left with her child.
There is no sorrowful song,
No possible symphony.
The shriek of the dirge would empty
The concert hall.

———————

I watched my friend suffer
When her child died.
And I knew that she would die
Though breathing
For the rest of her life.

The Larry Kramer

A documentary on Larry Kramer to be made.
I had to know him to choose filmed segments of his life.
He was sick and in hospital
And so I forced myself to make bedside visits.
This led to an adoration of
This gay icon
Who survived all the vulgarities of a liver transplant,
   HIV, and the maladies of eighty-one years of pas-
   sionate living.

Darling Larry, evolving into my muse.
Who woulda thought?
At first a stranger, with me at his bedside,
Telling him all my stories,
White lying about how good he looked.
He in gaga land of hoped recovery,
Occasionally bursting through with an insight.
"Pick your fight," he once said to me.
I had been asking him why he didn't move on from
   seeking a cure for AIDS.
"What about cancer?" I asked.

*How dare I ask him to change gears when his fight had
    saved so many lives?*
*How many men at how many events would bow down
    and thank him for saving their lives or their lovers
    or their friends?*
No Normal Heart,
This heroic man had the heart of Odysseus.

———————

*How could I tell this hero anything about life or any-
    thing else?*
Was he just tolerating me?
Was this fake familiarity?
*I was there because I had to know this man for this
    film.*
But I didn't expect to fall so madly in love.

———————

*I loved that he fought to get healthy, defying odds once
    again.*
I will not die, *he seemed to say.* I will not be forgotten,
    he seemed to say.
Yet death hovered and he was challenged.
*And then slowly, as if a miracle not to be believed, he
    got better.*

———————

*I loved that he looked forward to me and appreciated
    my visits.*
*We fell in love over a hospital bed as I fed him apple-
    sauce.*

"Have another spoonful," I begged. *"And I also brought*
  you an energy drink of papaya juice mixed with a
  raw egg."
"Oh, no, awful. Give it away," he said.
"But it says it will make you healthy."
"I'll get healthy without it," he said. *"But thank you."*
I played him show tunes on my iPad and we hummed
  and sang the lyrics we both knew.
I brought him headphones for hearing better. Even a
  birdcage to celebrate the first day of spring.
Once strangers, we friended over curious details.
Who wrote this, what plays were revivals, what was
  the zeitgeist?
There I was, a straight, once young, pretty docu-maker
With a great hero.
Both passing prime but raring to go.
I couldn't wait to see him each time
To watch his singular fight against impending death.
To see him marry his beloved David Webster.

———

We had nothing yet everything in common.
Raging insecurities.
He encouraged me to write some stories.
So I did.
And then I wrote more.
And he said they were good.

———

On many visits he would disclose that some other
  historical figure was gay.
He had proof.

"Mark Twain?"
"Oh, yes. He was a Clemens and used a pseudonym to
   hide his identity from his mother."
And then there was George Washington.
And then there was Honest Abe—not so honest.
And then, of course, Hamilton.
"Is there anyone who is straight?" I would ask, laughing.
Larry took this seriously.
I even began to wonder about myself.
I asked him, "What do you call a straight woman in
   love with a gay icon? A gay hetero?"
So, I laughed, it was now to be LGBTQ-GH.

———————

Love for me was Larry.
Once he suggested we run away to some
   island.
You see Larry was and is the most romantic man
   I have ever known.
He made me feel pretty no matter how wretched
   I looked.
Any visit would dissolve any of my headaches.
He would say he missed me
Adored me
Wanted my visits
That I lifted his spirits.
I felt a lover's vibrancy and that I was truly
   wanted.

———————

I have never been so inspired.
How dare I banter with a King?

I had heard he was cantankerous.
So I must be a worthy subject.
I had heard he was difficult.
Not at all with me.
I never found anything but courage,
Longing, love, respectability, genius.
Can you imagine this icon tremulous?
He continually questioned himself and his
    work.
And at the same time was brazen and brilliant.
Oh, that Larry.

———————

I was in an unusual place.
To be with him I was
Outed as special.
Surprised always by and en route to a mysterious
    moon.
I was an earthling entering something
Surreal.

———————

Larry is from the sky to my earth.
He lets me in and tells me to push on.
I bring him silently an invisible halo.

———————

Once I brought him an I Love NY hat.
He immediately put it on.
He appreciates.
His aura is inspiration.

Grant me more time.
Spare Larry and me more time.
I never displease him even when I displease myself.
He provides a lesson in parenting.

———————

Only once did I disappoint him, this master.
It was the day I mistook plain lox for Nova.
I accidentally brought him the cheaper kind of salmon.
He knew quality.
Nova was the truest of salmon offerings. How was I to
   know? Now I did.
Alas, I had failed him. All over a common salmon
   sandwich.
"Forgive me," I said. He did with a smile.
Never again cheap lox.

———————

But always again, I'll be there.
'Til next time.
I love you, Larry.
Thank you for being my unexpected, discovered-late-
   in-life love.

———————

You are a dream.
I am on your yacht.
We will sail.

Melissa Van Holdenvas

Melissa Van Holdenvas was twenty-two and well and
    properly educated.
She was pretty, they told her, but she never thought
    about it,
Guessing she was, and why not.
Losing her virginity out of curiosity, not passion,
She was in no hurry to find a beau.
And anyway, they always seemed to find her.

———————

There was one thing that turned her on, and it wasn't
    lust, it was ambition.
It was 1962 when determined women strived to be
    nurses. Melissa had no empathetic skills.
In addition, she hated blood,
So nursing was out,
Though she was clearly bloodthirsty.

———————

Melissa strived for a leading role in publishing.
She started as an apprentice editor.

Her job was essentially placing commas where needed,
Correcting spelling,
And verifying dates.
She was dutiful, but getting bored.
She had learned at an elite boarding school to be
    patient, and at an Ivy League college to trust timing.
But she felt a sense of urgency. Her patience was
    running out.
Her biological clock clicked-ticked "success now."

———————

Her job went on for two years with no hope for
    advancement.
One day she summoned up enough courage to see her
    boss and ask what her future might hold.
She called him Mr. Pennybroth. They rarely crossed
    paths.
She heard others call him Peter.
She would not dare such familiarity.
She had been told to use Miss or Mr. at her elite
    boarding school. (There was no Ms. as of that date.)
She made an appointment with Mr. Pennybroth's
    secretary, Gertie. (They were called secretaries then.)
Gertie was a character.
A woman about sixty with thick glasses.
"There's a space here Friday at six," Gertie said.
    "Take care, Melissa."
Melissa scarcely understood Gertie's caveat.
Hmm, take care, she thought.

One day, in the hottest of Julys,
The AC off as it was Fridays at 6 p.m.,
Melissa kept her appointment with Mr. Pennybroth
    and knocked carefully at his door.

"Come in," Mr. Pennybroth said.
Melissa opened the door quietly.
"Shall I shut it?" she asked.
And he said, "Yes, of course."

———————

"So you're Melissa Van Holden?" he continued, reading
*   it off a piece of paper.*
"Yes," Melissa said, not correcting his mistaking her
*   name.*
"You're a very good apprentice."
"Mr. Pennybroth," she blurted out, "I love my job and
*   I wondered if there was a future here, not that I*
*   would ever think of working anyplace else . . ."*
He smiled.
She was nervous, but well rehearsed.
"Call me Peter," he said. "Mr. Pennybroth sounds like
*   an old guy." He was certainly old to her—he was*
*   her father's age.*

———————

He stood up and said, "Let's talk about you, Miss
*   Melissa Van Holden."*
He had forgotten the "vas" again and she again chose
*   not to correct him.*
And so she moved to the couch, slippery leather, as
*   Peter Pennybroth sat closely next to her.*

———————

"You have very blue eyes, Melissa."
"Yes," Melissa said. "Our whole family. Dutch, you
*   know."*

"Ah, Dutch. I love tulips." And he sat with his arm
  around her close and then closer to her.
In the stifle of that moment,
Melissa found herself locked in an embrace with
  Mr. Pennybroth.
He grabbed her, kissed her, and then squeezed her.
Tightly.

———————

"Take care," Gertie had said.
Melissa Van Holdenvas now knew what Gertie had
  meant.
And she would "take care."
Melissa was on the pill and careful.
Mr. Pennybroth, now Peter, unbuttoned her blouse,
Put her hand on his fly,
And she unzipped it with care.

How could she?
How could she not!
It was hot.
She wanted more,
As did he.
If this is the road not taken, Melissa thought she'd take it.
And so she did.
Perfunctorily, perfected, punctuated—she
  acquiesced.
He was now Peter forever.
His passion was her purpose.

———————

Huffing and puffing, Peter and Melissa got it on.
Clothing off.

She knew exactly why and what.
He charged in,
She passionless.
Hump-Dee Dumpty.
Melissa left the office buttoned at exactly 7 p.m.

"Thank you, Mr. Pennybroth," she said knowingly.
"Thank you, Melissa Van Holden," said Peter Penny-
broth.
"It's Van Holdenvas," Melissa said. "You've been leav-
ing out the 'vas,'" correcting him while closing the
door gently.

And so, as was expected, early Monday morning
Gertie received written notice from Peter Penny-
broth that Miss Van Holden was no longer an
apprentice,
But an editor.
Gertie added the "vas" and Melissa knew what Gertie
knew and the rest of the office possibly knew, though
they dutifully congratulated her on her promotion.

It was 1962.
Practicing the safest of sex,
Melissa Van Holdenvas had taken care.
It was the launch of a stunning career.

A Day at Will

I HAD TO write a will today. Mine. Or at least revise an old boilerplate version I'd written years ago when dying was for other people. It was different now.

My lawyer was kind and gentle, no kid either. He helped me navigate the eventual disposal of my very self and all that I had acquired through years of toil and laborious sacrifice.

It was odd selecting various body parts for possible organ donations. Now, I am a very giving person when the hat is passed, but disposing of my corneas, kidneys, and heart, etc., all seemed exceedingly generous, even for me. I simply checked yes next to the give box. "Yes, indeed," I said, and quickly turned the page.

I was then to divide my small holdings, giving everything upon my death (or incapacitation) to my son, a son who never returns my calls. (He'll return this one when it happens, at least he'll know it's not me.) Some of my more psychically inclined friends think we'll always be in touch. I think I won't tell my boy that there's even a doubter's chance that such communication might occur.

Then came the question of my remains—my ashes, to be exact. I requested cremation. I don't cook and never have, but fortunately there are other people who do. Was I to be sprinkled, boxed, buried, or dusted off? I decided to leave this decision to my heirs. I simply couldn't make this judgment call and was somewhat relieved that I would never have to witness this familial event. Most decisions en famille have historically broken down into serious squabbles. I won't be there. I smiled. There are certainly some advantages to my non-beingness.

It then came time to sign and have witnessed this game plan for my exit. Two seemingly teenage legal assistants bolted into the office and witnessed without any evidence of pity my farewell manifesto. They were young and hopefully foolish, and signed as witnesses on the line with unwrinkled, unfreckled hands. They seemed anxious to get on with it, to get me over, so that they could go to lunch and continue with their lives. I thanked them without meaning it at all. How dare they be so cavalier about observing my termination. Time would pay them back. Of this I was sure.

I then bid adieu to my empathetic lawyer. As he walked me out he asked me if I found it a relief to get my lands in order. Feeling medieval, I agreed it was a great relief, responding by rote. Frankly, it was hideous.

Across the street from the scene of my imminent demise was an ice-cream creamery called Cold Stone. Truth. I entered full of joie de vivre and ordered with abandon. Possibly my last supper—an M&M sundae with hot fudge on peanut-butter ice cream topped with a mountain of whipped cream. I didn't need to fit into anything new, really, ashes or body; the coffins I know are one size fits all. However dark the day had been, it lit up with this ice-cream fiesta. Nothing could match this pleasure. No one was going to take this taste away from me. I was not giving away a morsel of my morsel. It was mine.

And then, as I left, I noticed they offered packed ice cream to go. And I thought of my little thirty-five-year-old baby boy. And so I took some for him—the same combo. I'd just drop it off, secretly place it in his freezer. I'm pretty sure no one will do something like this for him once I'm gone. And maybe it won't matter. Even if he never calls to thank me this time, I will always love him more than life itself.

Frenemy

Frenemy (*n*): an enemy pretending to be a friend.

———————

It is important to know who is your friend and who is your enemy.

It is especially important to know who is your frenemy, for this person can trip you up and land you in the wrong place.

So you must detect a frenemy and you must strive to never be one, except possibly for a brief time when it is necessary to be deceitful for your own immediate advantage.

If you frenemy too much it will soon get the best of you and you will not know who you really are and you will not know whom you really love.

As our friend St. Augustine said around A.D. 400, "Resentment is like taking poison and hoping the other person dies."

The same is true of seeking revenge.

Never destroy yourself in the search to destroy.

See a frenemy, but don't be a frenemy.

Now a frenemy is hard to detect.

They often seem really cozy and warm.

They pretend to see you as special, smart, and they sing your praises—when you're around.

They buy you too many gifts, often expensive. Why? To fool you into thinking that they like you. But in truth, they either want your job, possibly your husband—or just to trick you while they see you fail.

A frenemy can be of any age.

Don't be misled by youth or experience.

A frenemy is usually someone of your same sex.

Those stabs you feel along your back at night are not bedbugs.

The beast is your frenemy sticking pins in you silently.

And you must uncover this person.

By daylight a frenemy is sweetness and light. He or she joins the group of people who love you.

But be careful of brightness.

And don't be misled by bling.

Wear sunscreen.

There are also some frenemy discovery tips:

1. A frenemy works hard to leave you out. They will leave you out of discussions that would allow you to be on top of your game. You are always playing catch-up. For example: "I didn't know that, I wish I had known, no one told me . . ." Information from a frenemy is always a little late. A frenemy at the office will leave you off a CC. A frenemy will explain, "I thought I put you on it. You know me and computers."

2. A frenemy is overly concerned about you—at your slightest headache (while secretly hoping it's terminal), a frenemy will rush to you with aspirin, Advil, Tylenol, saying, "Oh, you poor baby." By then your headache will most likely have subsided.

3. *A frenemy is amazed at how young you look and will exclaim, "It is amazing how with every passing year, you look younger."*

4. *A frenemy exaggerates their own problems to evoke sympathy, kind of a Munchausen by Proxy frenemy syndrome. They work your sympathy for an imagined plight. They are crestfallen at a mole that they pretend they are sure is melanoma. They tell you the doctor is very concerned (they know it's a pimple). You must act worried; this is part of outsmarting them. But trust me, there is nothing to their ailments.*

5. *A frenemy does not think you are fat and you are.*

6. *Your frenemy thinks you will look beautiful with gray hair.*

7. *Be alert. For all their loving you and worrying about you, step carefully.*

You're on a slippery surface. Your shoes should have cleats. Because the bottom line is a frenemy is not that smart to think that you're not even smarter.

Now let's talk about friends.
A friend is a friend always.
They forget your weaknesses and remember your triumphs.
They pull away the fattening cookie.
They may even honestly forget your birthday. "Oh, shit, did you have another one already?"

A friend is a real treasure. Their lock of hair is always in your locket, and yours in theirs, whether you or they wear a locket or not.

A friend is close and special.

You tell your friend the truth, even if it hurts. And they respond honestly and tell it like it is.

A friend includes you in every detail that will make a difference.

They alarm you only when the chips are truly down.

They go with you to your second mammogram appointment or call you right after.

They're with you during that last walk when you say good-bye to a parent.

A friend goes to the mat for you.

Your dog loves them.

They never forget to bring your dog a bone.

Always remember to hold a friend close.

———————

P.S. Make sure that you make a notation in your Will that the frenemy, who can be named at this point, is not allowed to speak at your memorial service. Leave them out, no matter how tearful they are at your demise. Their moans and shrieks are for effect. This frenemy is deadly before the fact. Death is real and honest. Leave this most meaningful good-bye to friends alone.

Letter to a Dead Great-Aunt: A Personal Memoir

Great-Aunt Celia
Mount Zion Cemetery: Section 43
Queens, New York
United States of America

Dear Great-Aunt Celia,

It is nearly a hundred years since your tragic death in
the Triangle Shirtwaist Factory fire on March 25, 1911.
But it is just today that I discovered you really existed and
died in the infamous Triangle Fire. It hit me hard and
I cried for you and yet I never met you.

I had heard that Grandma Fanny's youngest sister had
died in the fire, yet it always seemed like family folklore.
My father was born some three years later. Occasionally
your death would come up in family conversations, but,
I am sorry to say, only briefly. Grandma Fanny's eyes
would tear up and then we would go on to hot chicken soup
or stuffed cabbage and some relative from the other side
would try to coax me to try some sweet-and-sour Russian
food that I had no interest in.

So here I am working on a documentary called
Schmatta. *The film is about the fall of the garment center
as a microcosm of the fall of Industrial America. The
producer mentioned immigrant labor and the fire. I said,
"I think I had a great-aunt who died in it."*

"Really," he said.

"Yes," I said.

"Well, there is a list of all who died," he said.

*"Oh," I said, "but I don't know my grandmother's
maiden name. She was born in Russia and she married my
grandfather there. I'll ask my uncle Seymour," I said. "My
father is dead. Uncle Seymour is my grandmother's only
living child."*

*"Uncle Seymour," I asked later that night, "did you
know Grandma Fanny's maiden name?"*

"Gittlin," he said without hesitation.

"G-I-T-L-I-N," I spelled.

"No, two ts."

*"And what was her dead sister's name, the one who died
in the fire?"*

*"I don't know," Uncle Seymour said. "But my name was
supposed to be like hers."*

*Uncle Seymour is sharp as a tack at eighty-four; he says
his grief-stricken mother left the United States several
months later to go to Belarus because she had to tell her
mother, Lypska, that her youngest daughter was dead.
There were only telegraph wires then, Grandma spoke only
Yiddish, and no one in the Western Union telegraph office
understood how to write it. Regardless, she was convinced
her mother would die if she was alone when she found out
Celia was dead. So, Grandma Fanny took the nine-day
trip back to Russia. My uncle said she didn't know she was
two months pregnant with my father. Neighbors on the
Lower East Side had collected money for her trip and she
gave birth to my father in Russia. She stayed with her*

mother for two years before returning to America. Pogroms had broken out in Belarus and Grandma Fanny and her newborn son hid in her mother Lypska's grocery-store basement for two years. For reasons Uncle Seymour didn't know, his grandmother died during her daughter Fanny's stay. Maybe it was grief over your death that killed your mother. Who knows?

That's the history, Celia; your history as best we can tell it. Your mother mourned you. The factory listed you as Selina Gittlin, but we knew at the morgue that it was our Celia Gittlin. On the death certificate it was correct— Celia from Clinton Street. You spoke no English. Neither did anyone in the family. Immigrants' names were up for grabs.

Dear Aunt Celia, you died at seventeen. The fire was on the twenty-fifth of March. Did you lie there suffering on Greene Street? Did you die immediately? Did your corpse lie alone on the curb? The death notice said your skull was fractured. Did you jump? Of course, your sister Fanny got you the job at the shirt factory in America. She summoned you from Russia and said that you could be rich someday and meet a good man in America. She said you could share their one-room apartment at 174 Clinton Street until your prince came to save you. There was plenty of room for you there—it was a big room. The bathtub was in the kitchen but don't worry; it had a curtain for privacy.

You came alone on a ship in early November 1910. You brought a samovar and a small sewing machine. The samovar wound up with me. I have it. I never asked where it came from. Now I know.

I wish I could have met you at Ellis Island. If only for a moment, for you died five months later—that's what it says on your death certificate. Aunt Celia, did you try the doors? Were you trampled by other women? Did you jump *from the window because the exit doors were locked so the working girls couldn't smoke? Did you smoke? You were just a little girl. Who taught you to sew? I'm left-handed and terrible at sewing. Do I look like you? Did you think any of the thoughts I thought at seventeen? What did you pack for lunch that day? Could you ever forgive your sister, my grandma Fanny, for bringing you to America? Did you walk to work that day? A sixteen-hour workday. A seven-day workweek. Were you tired that Saturday or did you think you were lucky to have a job in this shirt sweatshop? I want to know. And I want you to know how sad I am that you died so young. Was it scary alone on the boat to America? Did the sewing machine and samovar smell of Old Russia? Were you proud to go to your new job? Did you audition for the Triangle boss with your Russian sewing machine? Did you ever know love? You were certainly beloved.*

Celia, I mourn for you, for the lack of safety and the treatment of immigrants. I am outraged and panicked when a crane kills a worker, or there is a senseless fire in a nightclub, or an immigrant is ruthlessly deported; for I, your grandniece, am the child of immigrants. My father was born in Russia.

Celia, I think I see the ghost of you. I see the babushka pulling back your kinky long hair so that it won't be caught in the sewing machine. Uncle Seymour's name is like yours, Uncle Sey-mour, Ce-lia. We feel you, Celia, in our hearts as a relative who owns a piece of our being. Sheila-Celia.

I visit your grave at Mount Zion Cemetery and place a stone for you from all of us. I'm not religious, but I believe in remembering. I want to tell you how sorry I am that you lost your life. My heart aches for you and all the young immigrant girls who lost their lives for greed on that day in

March . . . March 25, 1911, the Triangle Shirtwaist Factory fire.

May all of you rest in peace.
With all my love,
In Memory,
Fondest,
Your grandniece, Sheila

A Million-Dollar Smile

I HAVE SPENT more on my teeth (most of us have thirty-two) than on any of my weddings, expensive spa vacations, or my kid's entire education.

This toothy madness began in preadolescence, when I wore braces for some three years for a slight overbite, which I owed to prolonged thumb sucking. This frontal bucking created a mouth made for remolding. My mother had wanted a perfect child and so I was rushed to an NYU dental clinic where trembling dental wannabes completed their education in my less-than-perfect mouth.

Actually, I was all for this renovation because Stanley (heart-throb) Brettschneider wouldn't kiss me in the closet during my first hot game of spin the bottle. (I was almost twelve.) In this earliest of traumas, Stanley told me, quite frankly, that he didn't kiss girls with braces and rubber bands. It was too dangerous. I was devastated and waited impatiently for the corrected-perfected me. Yet, alas, when the metal and rubber were removed, Stanley had moved to the burbs, and we never did kiss. But that was years ago and my poor-girl braces kept my smile going for some thirty years—maintaining at bargain prices a rich girl's smile, in a poor girl's clinically improved mouth.

But things do happen, and one day in my forty-somethingth year—a man-eating pain struck my left canine. Yelping wolflike,

I called my family dentist (very sweet Dr. Sweder) and began a winding dental path of new discovery.

Dr. Sweder arranged for me to meet, on a bloody Sunday in April, a well-paid drill sergeant named Dr. Bain. He was known professionally as an endodontist—a new word had entered my vocabulary. I was an endodontic emergency and after some ten thousand X-rays, Dr. Bain introduced me to the root-canal experience, a journey I would grow accustomed to. With a rubber towelette and wee guillotine equipment, a sadist's drill and a twisting motion, he would remove an infected nerve from my tooth, which was attached to my gum, which was attached to my mouth, which was attached to me. What had led Dr. Bain to do this gyrating turn of the screw? Possibly it was better not to know.

Dr. Bain played opera and whistled while he worked. Each time he pierced and pulled, he asked me if I liked a particular opera and I always grunted—*ah, huh, eh, huh*—for words were impossible during root-canal incarceration and it seemed foolhardy to disagree with someone who practiced mouth S and M. Anyway, I am not an opera fan. I believe it was he, Dr. Bain, who started me on the costly dental smile train. An express with no local stops. Even my four-year-old son, who cracked a tooth, was referred by him to a pedodontist. The pedodontist was a bit scary at first, but I was assured he was not a felon, but a trained specialist in baby teeth. Phew. And then through Dr. Bain's associations I became acquainted with the prosthodontist, who introduced me to the periodontist, who introduced me to the oral surgeon.

You see, no one dentist would tend to a whole tooth. My tooth was fragmented. The profession of saving teeth had become a fine art. Nowhere was there to be found a plain, simple, do-it-all dentist anywhere, anyplace. Nary a month went by when I didn't pay a visit to be bled, capped, or implanted by some relative of the dental family tree. I was treated by professional men with specific expertise. Their bills were fast and furious, the coverage limited; but, oh, what a smile I was earning—rather, they were earning. I would show my porcelains off like a college girl with an expensive engagement ring. Showtime.

In retrospect, you have to feel sorry for these guys. I think I have discovered the secret to the closely knit society of dentists. When visiting the gynecologist or even the proctologist, with legs in the stirrups, or arse up, you can still engage in dialogue about the world or tell a story, or at least respond to questions like, "Do you like *La Traviata*?" Not so in a dental chair. Tilted, swathed, poked with sharp tools, drilled at, water spouting in your eye—all you can do is make guttural sounds like *ugh, ah, err, uhm, eh.*

Grandma put her teeth in a jar. She, too, had a beautiful smile, though artificial, and not firmly planted. And though Grandma's teeth occasionally made themselves known by a loose click that would disturb a family conversation, this was a rare occasion and would only occur when there was a seismic shift of plates. It was quickly Fixodented by her. But Grandma had one dentist: our family dentist, dear Dr. William B. Sweder. He knew us. He was my very first dentist. He used to calm me. He gave me balloons. We all liked to see him. He filled my first tooth. He said it wouldn't hurt, and it didn't. He fluoridated me. He told me about the Tooth Fairy (she worked on his behalf). He also gave me free toothpaste and a brush with a clown's head. And Dr. Sweder did it all—from baby teeth on, from day one to dentures—the beginning to the end. He knew us all. But he's long gone. I miss him. But, unlike Grandma, I do keep my teeth in at night—for the hefty price of being on the smile train. Without question, I do have a million-dollar smile. And I'm not speaking metaphorically.

Eunice's Period.
Stopped.

Eunice remembered the day she got her Period.
Yippee.
'Cause she was late and nearly thirteen.
Some friends would blush about it all,
but on her red-banner day,
Eunice brazenly entered Murphy's Pharmacy.
"A box of Kotex," she said, loudly—proudly,
"and a belt with pins for sanitation napkins."
"Congratulations, Eunice," said Mr. Murphy.
For in the small town in which she lived,
Eunice's mother, Agnes McAdams, had clearly
    shared
this awaited late arrival with
Mrs. Alice Murphy,
who had shared it with Mr. Douglas Murphy,
her balding kindly pharmacist husband of some forty
    years.
Doc Murphy knew what ailed everyone in town,
from prescriptions, gossip, and his own homespun
    advice.

———————

Time would pass
without asking,
and
some forty years later, when
the Murphys were long gone,
and the lone pharmacy dissolved into a chain of cold
    chemists,
Eunice's mother, Agnes McAdams, died quickly—cancer.
And Eunice's period stopped just as abruptly.

———————

It stopped flowing through her.
Eunice would longingly look at the Tampax box
knowing that of the thirty-six she bought on sale
some thirty-four would now go to waste.
But for nostalgia's sake
she held on to them
for her daughters, a visitor, but never for herself
again.
And she questioned with this sudden stoppage.
Was she useful to the universe
without the hot-blooded reminder of fecundity?
She wondered.

———————

Did this cessation equate with purpose?
Would she ever again feel the urge to be close to a
    man?
Would her recent divorce and celibacy in menses
cause the ebb of her physical longing?

Yet oddly,
as the months passed,
she recovered heroically as in the days of "Kotex,
    please."
And a new life force began to flow through her.
Sometimes hot, sometimes erotic, sometimes sweaty
    with anxiety
she would grow to treasure the beat of her new
    being.
For she was equal now in Woman Power
to Man Power.
She would no longer anticipate the dreaded PMS
or
run out of plugs in the middle of . . .
Nor worry about pregnancy
or stains or wearing very white
or feel estranged from the Peter principle,
for a new fierce self emerged
a female self in a man's world.
Adieu to estrogen,
bon voyage.
Good riddance.
No balms or pills to restore what was lost
for she had found a drive
moving forward
to being older.
A graying woman forthright though blond
a rara avis* to herself.
For Eunice would spread her plumage,
a palette of feathers

---

n., pl.* ra·ra avis·es or ra·rae aves (râr'ē ā'vēz). A rare or unique person or thing. [Latin rāra avis : **rāra, feminine of **rārus**, rare+avis, rare bird.]

sans red
burning brightly, a kaleidoscope changing,
glorious and necessary,
lustful and powerful with infinite possibilities
as ever and more.

———————————

Did You Ever See a Book Cry?

DID YOU ever see a book cry?
　　Well, I did.

On the red-eye flight returning from L.A., the lights from the digital screens were glowing—it was 2 a.m. The iPads, Galaxies, iPhones, and Kindles were lighting up with their digital messages, giving the cabin an eerie aura.

So there I was in the midst of this *now-age* flight, reading a hardcover book. It dated me. Like saying "record" when you mean "MP3." Or "telephone" when you mean "cell." But I didn't care.

Suddenly a strange thing occurred. In the midst of a rather disturbing turbulent bump, my hardcover book's eyes opened (I didn't know until that very moment that books had eyes). Suddenly tears rolled down on the book's cover and the book spoke. "I'm over," it said, sobbing, "done for. Everything is digital, I'm black and white. I'm old-fashioned print. They discount me in supermarkets, sell coffee and knickknacks in bookstores just to keep me breathing. I have no mom-and-pop shops anymore to keep me feeling like I have a home. I'm an artifact, a dinosaur. I've lost my bookmark. I'm a mere smudge."

Alarmed at this emotional, paranormal weeping, I whispered to my book, "Please don't cry. I love you. I love the way you feel. I love the way you pack in my suitcase. You have no glass that can shatter. I love the way your last page feels and always keeps me waiting and your first page that invites me in. I loved you when you were a Bible or Shakespeare or Dostoyevsky. No Kindle could light that fire. I loved you when you were *A Tree Grows in Brooklyn* and some thousand pages of *Vanity Fair*. I loved you when my fingers turned your pages. Even when I couldn't read, I loved you as a picture book. Nothing could compare to the way it felt when I could pat my bunny from *Pat the Bunny*. For me, dearest book, you are eternal and always unique."

"Alas," the book sobbed, "I'll never be a valuable first edition again. No one will collect me. No one will ever treasure my physical existence as they once did."

Without anyone looking, I wiped the book's tears away and kissed it gently. "You will always be special to me," I whispered. "And one day when they whack and hack the Internet into nonexistence and all the lights go out all over the world and everyone is stranded, you and me babe, we'll be together. We'll light a simple candle and read our paper map to eternal safety."

The book's tears stopped and its eyes miraculously disappeared into its jacket.

No one will ever know what happened in the sky at 32,000 feet. I tilted my seat backward, closed my eyes, and hugged my dear hardcover book, while clutching it to my heart.

Advice to Women in a Male-Dominated Workplace

THE FOLLOWING rules were written by Ms. Meredith Wilson, former senior vice president at a leading women's magazine. After twenty-six years of dutiful service, she was fired in five minutes and told by Human Resources to vanish immediately, as her replacement—an expert in digital technology—was soon to arrive. The magazine was to go exclusively digital.

These ten rules below were posted on every women's bathroom door of the twenty-story building, presumably left by SVP Wilson as she left the office for the last time. Below is the only remaining salvaged copy, the rest having been disposed of within minutes of their posting.

Advice to Women in a Male-Dominated Workplace (by a Woman Who Knows)

Rule #1—Some say lean in. Sure. Try it. But that tilt usually, in spite of its current popularity, can land you flat on your fanny—or better yet, flat on your face.

Leaning in and knowing when to lean in is a question
of timing. It's an instinct and a talent you are either
born with or have to develop.

Rule #2—Learn to flatter.
Say, "You really do think of others."
Or/and/et cetera, et cetera, et cetera, "How do you
find time to be Principal of the Day?"
Play these roles well. Fine acting skills are essential.
Take acting lessons if you must and take them
seriously. All of these rules require exquisite dramatic
dexterity.

Rule #3—Learn to assure your boss/bosses that you
have mastered the art of having it all. Practice saying,
"I have great home care and easy kids of course and
I'm free to go anywhere and at any time of the day or
night."

Rule #4—Learn to look as good as you can.
Schedule regular Botox if you are of a certain age. Just
enough, please.
Blowouts are a necessity and blonde streaks never hurt
anyone.
And never admit to feeling creaky or old.
Also—you are never to be sick!
Menstrual cramps do not cramp, menopause never
happens.
The temperature is always perfect in the boss's office.

Rule #5—Learn to laugh at jokes—especially if they're
not funny. Never tell a topper.
Learn the art of saying, "Mr. So-and-So, that is ha-ha-
hilarious!"

Rule #6—Learn to never admit you already know
something you already know. Say something like,
"That's so interesting. I didn't know that. I should
have known that."

Rule #7—Learn not to have true feelings. Though
your heart may be broken, memorize this line, "I
don't mind at all, it's your call."
Again with feeling. "I don't mind at all, it's your call."
Save your tears for your pillow.

Rule #8—Learn to not ask directly for more money
but mention "en passant" that a fellow male employee,
at your level, got a well-deserved raise and you were
very happy for him.

Rule #9—Learn to network.
You never know when your time may be up. For your
bosses can dispose of you with the shortest notice and
with the shortest of good-byes. Remember there is
always competition. So be sure to meet your company's
competitors far from your office and be certain they
know of your good works.

Rule #10—Learn the art of the insincere thank-you.
Act like you owe your employer everything. But know
that the truth is they owe *you* everything.

*Following these rules will land you in the best possible
position to succeed. They will serve you well.*
*But remember the fact is that the very top belongs to the
womb-less—not the wo-men.*
Speak your mind—but remember only half of it.

Save the best for lasting . . . in your job.
Face it head on.
Chin up.
You're in the army now.

> *With my best wishes,*
> *Meredith Wilson*
> *Former Senior Vice President*

Do You Believe in Santa Claus?

I DIDN'T BELIEVE in Santa Claus as a child, but now I do. Well, actually I did believe fervently in Santa Claus until I was six. But I had certain specific questions. I lived in an apartment building in New York City and found it hard to imagine him coming down the chimney, since this chimney serviced some one hundred apartments and some two hundred children. My mother told me that that was why Santa left a large black garbage bag filled with toys outside apartment 4A on Christmas morning. My wicked friend Eileen, who was seven, told me there was no Santa Claus and that I was stupid to believe that he was real. I hated her for this reality check, but it did get me thinking. Like, where were the reindeer, especially Rudolph? And how did Santa Claus drop gifts off for all the good kids first in my building and then in the world? And who was that man outside St. Patrick's Cathedral ringing a bell, when down the street at the Rockefeller Center skating rink there was another Santa whose white beard was askew, revealing dark stubble? It didn't add up.

And so I asked my mother, "Mom, is Santa for real or are you the real Santa? Does Santa really live at the North Pole or does he sometimes sit in a chair at Macy's? Tell me the truth, Mom."

And Mom answered, "All you have to do is believe in him and say he is and he is. You say he is true because he brings you toys, so it is best to believe."

And that's why at this advanced age I decided to write to Santa, because I believe he lives at the North Pole and is a good man with good motives and I owe him kind regards.

Dear Santa,

Thank you for giving me so many good gifts when I was a child. The last gift I remember was a pair of red ice skates. Uncle Bot (short for his last name which was Botwinik) used to take me ice-skating and we would whirl around Wollman Rink in Central Park. Uncle Bot was eighty-eight and Aunt Diana, his wife, said that one day Uncle Bot would just die in the rink. She warned us both, but we twirled anyway. As luck would have it, Uncle Bot would die a year later on the IRT, going to work at eighty-nine. And Santa (would you believe this?), Aunt Diana blamed it on Bot. She said that if he had taken a taxi and didn't have to climb the stairs to the subway, he would be alive today. But Uncle Bot loved the train. I miss Uncle Bot.

I tell you all this today because I never really told you enough about myself or how close certain things were to my heart. I believe I have never really thanked you for the years of toys, for the skates, for all the gifts for the children rich and poor, and for the many spiritual things that might not fit exactly in your bag.

So thank you, Santa, for my most adorable son and for my all-suffering husband. Thank you, Santa, for allowing me to realize my talents and for giving me good friends and a salary that helps me get pretty things for myself and a position in life that allows me to receive gifts from others, although I am known to re-gift many of them. Thank you,

Santa, for helping me face my existential existence by allowing me to carry a tune well, which permits me to sing out loud and feel better on days when I think life has no meaning. And thank you, Santa, for giving me time on this troubled planet to dance if I choose to, even though I can only wear flats since gravity has made the balls of my feet hurt.

Thank you, Mr. Claus, for making me believe in the magic of loving and knowing I can care for people and people can care for me more than a million. I know, although it is not a proven fact, that you exist. That you will, nonetheless, always be at the North Pole for all children and for all time, and that gives me great comfort. Please keep warm and thanks for loving Mrs. Claus, even though she's chubby. Always remember me as one of your good children, now grown up and oldish.

And I wonder, embarrassing as it may sound, I wonder if it would be possible if you could bring me a new pair of Uggs—the brownish golden ones that you can fold down so the alpaca lining shows. (If they have to kill the llama, scratch the alpaca.)

As my mother told me, I can't see any reason not to believe in you. All I have to do is say you are and therefore you will be. As far as I can see, there's no downside.

To you, Mrs. Claus, the elves, Rudolph, and all the other reindeer, Merry Christmas!

All my love,
Your good child

The Cookie Wars:
W.M. vs. Mrs. Spatz

THE FANCY private school for boys announced to the third-grade mothers that next Tuesday there would be a Mommies' Bake Sale. The time? One o'clock in the afternoon—perfect for working mothers, right? Most of the mothers in this elite school did not work. They had made a decision to be stay-at-home moms and would often say to this Working Mom, known hereafter as W.M., "I don't know how you do it!" Many were supportive of W.M.'s crazy work schedule, sometimes picking up and taking her son to special midday events. Mrs. Wasserstein even complimented W.M. on her work's recognition. "You are something else," she said. "You have it all." To which W.M. replied, "Hardly," while scratching a miserable body rash attributed to tension and anxiety.

One exception to any form of kindness, though there may have been more at-home mommies of her kind lurking, was Mrs. Spatz—the president of the Mommies' Association. She had evil planted in her DNA, possibly passed down from generations of snobbery. But more on that later . . .

Inside the gym-sale cookie extravaganza, many busy nine- and some just-ten-year-old boys would be wearing their expensive uniforms—little Brooks Brothers blue jackets with their little gold school emblems. These third-graders would be allowed to collect money by selling their mommies' cookies. All of these jackets would certainly be outgrown by the next year, requiring the Mommies' Association to contribute the barely worn, pricey, separatist uniforms to those poor, less fortunate boys mostly living in the "other" part of the city.

The proceeds from this cookie event were for the library in this private school, which presented itself as desperately in need of cash for new books. *Really?* thought W.M. Given the tuition and other additional monies requested during the school year, it hardly seemed necessary to W.M. that Mommy-as-Baker would be providing needed cash. But it was a way, said Mrs. Spatz, to teach the boys the value of hard work and money. *Oh, please,* W.M. thought to herself. Deep down W.M. believed it was just a way for Mrs. Spatz to inconvenience the few working mothers. Mrs. Spatz also refused to be called "Ms." She carried herself with the dignity and finesse of an outdated oligarch. "Ms. is for manuscript," she once told W.M., to which W.M. replied, "It can be. But not in my case."

W.M. went along with the Spatz ruse for the sake of her little boy, whom she believed was getting a superior education with field trips and third-grade Latin. She herself had never had such privileges and, as parents will do, wanted more for her son.

Rushing out of work at midday, W.M. ran to Mrs. Fields, an exclusive cookie store that was located in her office building. She asked for a dozen various cookies—peanut butter, macadamia, chocolate chip, and even one with sprinkles. She politely rushed the poor saleslady, who was meticulously wrapping each cookie. "Ms.," W.M. said. "I'm really sorry but I'm in a hurry and so appreciate your care, but just toss them in the box, please." But the saleslady insisted that Mrs. Fields's detailed training required this careful wax-paper wrap.

"That's all right," W.M. said hastily. "Just give me the box." W.M. grabbed the box and fled with some cookies wrapped and some tossed. Mrs. Fields was clearly not a working-mother-baker, or maybe she once was, who knows? Maybe this Mrs. Fields was just a Nabisco front for some conglomerate.

W.M. was gone, dashing to the subway, running east to the 6 train. She arrived at the private school at 1:10 p.m.

Her little boy in his Brooks Brothers jacket said, "You're late, Mom."

"I rushed! I rushed, sweetie. Here I am!" W.M. replied. She ran up breathless to Mrs. Spatz. "Mrs. Spatz," W.M. said. "I'm so sorry I'm late."

Little boys in their emblematic jackets were lined up behind a long table and were selling cookies to their own moms who had themselves donated Mommy's cookies, which were bought by other mommies who had donated their Mommy's cookies. *This cookie madness is monstrous*, W.M. thought. To W.M., the lack of economic profit was apparent, as mostly rich kids raised money that wasn't needed for the library that was perfectly well funded. But per Mrs. Spatz's memorandum, the boys were to feel useful during this useless barter. No wonder by the time they got to middle school, there appeared to be a growing drug problem.

Mrs. Spatz looked at the Mrs. Fields box of cookies. "Are these your cookies?" she asked W.M. "Or just Mrs. Fields's?"

"They're my cookies," W.M. said. "I bought them at Mrs. Fields."

Mrs. Spatz did not smile. "I'm so sorry," she said. "This sale is for mommies who baked their own cookies."

"But what difference does it make?" asked the harried W.M. She had run to the school not having had time for lunch and felt a little woozy.

"It makes a difference," said Mrs. Spatz, "that the boys know their *mothers* made the cookies."

"A cookie is a cookie," said W.M.

"Still, it is the spirit of the thing," said Mrs. Spatz.

W.M. tried to control her fury. "I bet," she said as gently as she could, "that most of these are baked by nannies at home anyway."

"Yes, maybe," said the determined Mrs. Spatz. "But they're not store-bought."

"What difference does that make?" said W.M. "A mommy may have made them in a store."

"Yes," insisted Mrs. Spatz, "but she would not have been a mommy from *this* school."

W.M. was silent. Her little boy started to cry. "Why didn't you bake them or have Rosarie bake them?" he asked.

W.M. answered, "Because, sweetheart, I thought buying these expensive cookies was a better way to do this. I'm sorry," she said. "I didn't know they meant only homemade-by-Mommy."

The buzz of selling and the smell of cookies filled the auditorium, which had turned into a bizarre bazaar.

"Mrs. Spatz," W.M. said pleadingly. "Is there any way my son can still have some part in this wonderful event?" She tried to sound sincere.

"Well," Mrs. Spatz said, "I suppose he can bag them."

W.M. wiped away her son's tears. Fifty small brown paper bags were provided to W.M.'s son and he put each cookie sale in a separate bag, as the other kids sold and wrapped proudly, earning money from this ridiculous exchange and putting the profits in a painted shoebox carefully scrolled LIBRARY FUND. Mrs. Spatz, with her exquisite sense of solidarity, had even placed the school's emblem on the box.

W.M.'s boy worked diligently. An outcast, but at least part of the fray. W.M. was beside herself as she watched this façade. After an hour, the total profit was announced triumphantly by Mrs. Spatz. "You boys," she said, "should be proud," she said, "for your hard work," she said, "and all you've achieved," she said. "You have raised," she said, "a glorious," she said, "one hundred and fifty-seven dollars," she said, "for your school's library." And then to top it off, the most likely underpaid school librarian said how deeply grateful she was for the contribution to the library, which had always been stocked full with generous donations from the alumni fund.

A hundred and fifty-seven fucking homemade cookies were sold at a dollar apiece. W.M. was furious at the charade but could not lose her cool. Mrs. Spatz was Primo Mommo. Getting on her bad side would reflect badly on any kid whose mother was not in Spatz's favor. A mom opposing Mommo might suddenly lose a birthday party invite for her child, or worse—upcoming sleepover opportunities. So W.M. was silent. You see, Mrs. Spatz's husband was a significant donor to the school. He had been a student there himself and was now a successful banker in his father's firm, which he had inherited.

So before returning her son to class, W.M. and her little boy broke the strings on the box of Mrs. Fields cookies. Each took a cookie, she the one that had lost its sprinkles. Plain, bare, but honest.

"Sorry I didn't bake you Mommy's cookies so you could sell your own," she told her son.

"That's okay, Mom. Some of the kids bought back the cookies their own mommies had baked. Isn't that stupid?" he observed.

"Yes, it is, isn't it," she said. Her little boy was no dope. "Thanks, sweetie," W.M. said, "Kiss, please. I have to go back to work now."

"Bye, Mom."

"Bye, sweetheart. Want another cookie?" she asked.

"No," he said, smiling. "It isn't homemade by my mommy." And then he cracked up. She was relieved. "But, Mom, could you get me the new Gameboy 2? I need to play Tetris. I really need to."

"You really need it?"

"Yes. I need it," he said.

Blackmail accepted, W.M. thought. A small price to pay.

"I'll stop in at Toys 'R' Us on the way home," she assured him.

And she knew from this clever banter and barter that she had permission to be a working mom and that the price was not a homemade cookie. And she knew even better that her little boy, now almost ten, would survive in a brutal world, for he had proved during the Cookie Wars to be street smart and wise and that he would take no prisoners.

Mentor Not

Mentor, you ask?
Oh, please.
Someone, man or woman, who took me by the hand
  and showed me the right way?
Come on.
No, never ever.
No gushing moonie here who saw the light via a guid-
  ing guru.

———————

Certainly idols—Eleanor Roosevelt, Gloria Steinem,
  the Greek goddess Athena, Helen Gurley Brown for
  cleavage, and Madame Bovary for sacrifice.

———————

But really my finest mentor was revenge.

———————

I was madly in love at Yale.
The boy was at Harvard Law.

We met in moot court. Yale vs. Harvard.
I played Ethel Rosenberg. She was on trial for being a
*   Communist spy with her husband.*
She was turned in by her brother-in-law.
It was fun to play this part with this handsome Har-
*   vard Law student defending me.*
I wanted him to be my boyfriend.
Your Honor, I was guilty.
Guilty of first love.
He was too. It was instant.
We turned Boston into New Haven and New Haven
*   into Boston.*
My love had blue eyes and straight blond hair.
I had immigrant status and kinky locks.
His lineage going back to icons of early America.
His Colony Club status vs. my Girl Scout badge.
His Jesus and my Moses.

———————

He wrote me poetry.
He painted pictures of me with balloons that said "love."
He adored me—I believe that regardless.
I would sneak him into the girls' dorm, not letting him
*   go until morning.*
Down the back stairway.
Please let it last.
There was nothing like it.
No movie, no love song, no poem could capture this
*   romance.*

———————

I believed there was a heaven and that I had gone to it.
For one whole school semester we were inseparable.

*I imagined life with him in a field of daisies and
        dissolving kisses*
Made of ether and lilac.
Trance. I was in a trance and I believed he was too.

My friends warned me.
He was too rich.
Too establishment.
Too entitled.
*My dad was a mailman who had a sideline of booking
        bets at the post office.*
*My mom, ill and struggling, was an active cardholding
        member of the Communist party.*
*We used to wait until the notice came to pay the prior
        month's rent.*
*Grandma and Grandpa, always quarrelling, lived
        with us.*

But this love punched me dizzy.
It twirled me out of my day-to-day.
Let's call him "The Love of my Life" for cover.
Reality brought it down.
*This crash of a broken heart took decades to recover
        from.*
As I write fifty years later it aches fresh.

---

*He took me to his home—a historic family house pre-
        served in fancy Connecticut.*
I met his mother the last weekend of the school year.

Please like me. I love your son 'til ever . . .
I was nervous.
The silverware had family initials.
They said grace before dinner.
I did not know the world I was in or the words they
    would say.
"Bless us, O Lord, and these Thy gifts . . ."
Please, Lord, save me.
His father drove a Jaguar.
We had a used Dodge Dart.

———————

Gilbert Stuart's paintings hung on the walls.
Relatives from long ago stared at me.
His family in the pictures nodded. No no, little poor
    girl, no no.
Not here, not now, not ever.
I did not belong with this social elite.
Wrong label. Wrong fabric. Wrong design.

———————

And then as his mother and I dried the dishes—
    good little girl, pretty little girl, nervous little
    girl me.
Blue-book mother, she asked me the question made of
    tradition and prejudice.
"Sheila, dear," she said, *"aren't you Jewish?"*
"Yes," I said.
"So," she said. *"Aren't there any interesting Jewish men*
    at Yale who would be more suitable for you?"
Yes, yes, yes. She did say that.
I hardly knew what to say.

Was it just anti-Semitism?
Was it a question with an answer?
I can't remember if I answered.

―――――――

I choked back tears.
I wanted to go home.
I want to tell you reading this that I answered her.
But I was too stunned to say anything.
Numb, I remember.
I could not feel.
I'd like to tell you I walked out and walked
    away.
But I think I smiled and continued to dry the dishes.
    I took it.
That I remember.

―――――――

So let's say mentor who?
She—this blue-blooded archetype defending her uncir-
    cumcised son.
She is my mentor.
None better.
This mother who deemed me unworthy
Has been by my side through
Accolades for accomplishment,
Praise for good deeds.

―――――――

Every trophy was for her.
Every yes to me was a slap in her face.

Every yes was a talk back.
It said, "I was worthy of your son."
I would win for her.
I received my prizes in retribution.
Die, lady, die,
Stick your finger in your eye,
Tell your son that it was I
Feast your loss in my clear brown eyes.
For I was not bold enough then.

———————

You deferred my dream.
His dream too, or so
I would like to think.
She is my mentor, churning,
Long dead, I imagine.
She is the ghost of yesteryear.
Sometimes she is still with me as a driving force.
She is my revenge.
All I did was to prove her wrong.
Her condemning spirit often lets me edit late at night
*   without fatigue.*
I dress in clothes she would not approve of.
But I approve.
She shops with me and says, "No no, not
*   tasteful."*
Her red lipstick is my preferred pink punk.
She motivates me to succeed.
The wolf may have licked his lips when he swallowed
*   Little Red Riding Hood,*
But she outsmarted him and came out whole—safer
*   and wiser.*
I am Little Red Riding Hood.

As for her son,
He drove me back to the dorm after that night.
We kissed for the last time.
A forever good night.
I knew I would never see him again.
He would follow the family game plan.
His mother's ditto-boy.
Gilbert Stuart long dead, had painted his portrait a
    hundred years before he was born.
I was a Polaroid then.
I knew he would swim with the prevailing tide.
I would love him forever anyway,
For the gift never opened was a gift I cherished, sadly.

———————

His cowardice, my honor guard.
You do not choose who will break your heart.
Revenge is the only balm.

———————

Here I am successful on my own.
Here are all my trophies.
Today they are all for me.
Thank you.

———————

I will never forgive you, fancy-lady-land.
You were wrong about me from the get-go.
I would win the race as a long shot.
I try to forget you.

And you fade.
Thanks for the mentoring.
I see myself in the lead and you behind.
Yes, revenge was the driving force.
I go faster.
I left you and your son at the gate.
I can never ever thank you enough for the pain and the
*   purpose.*
This story is now mine.
All mine.

The Day She Lost
Her Jealousy at Barneys

S HE HAD always been slightly envious of other girls. It started with doll clothes in third grade. Marylou's doll had high heels and a bikini swimsuit. Hers did not. This competitive nature continued, with more serious manifestations, into high school. At the elegant Pierpont High, she longed for Ginger's blue eyes and Margaret Gullen's knees. The fancy girls' high school required dark blue knee socks with the dark blue uniform. Margaret's knees, or so it appeared to her, were dimpled in all the right places—whereas hers appeared to her to be knobby, almost swollen. As for Ginger, once you stared into her blue eyes you never looked down. For Ginger, knees were irrelevant.

As she grew into adulthood, she did so with jealousy nipping at her heels—always wanting something or someone she didn't have. Disposing of husbands, estranging her children, she was never satisfied. She wanted her best friend Corrine's husband, and when he left Corrine, she got him for a night—and she couldn't wait to get rid of him. Yes, he could certainly get it up, but it wouldn't go down. She was exhausted. She never told Corrine. And then she wanted Aretha's job—but Aretha got fired and soon after the company she worked for went bankrupt and went under. Then she wanted Peggy's family fortune, but Peggy's father disowned his daughter when she took a Latino lover and produced a dark-skinned heir to the DuPont fortune.

And so her longing to be somewhere or someone else faded. She began to look to herself for the answers, to create the illusion that she was perfect—a canvas on which to paint the perfect other her. She was the first to the bar, with tummy tuck, face-lift, brow lift, thigh lipo, lip plumping, veneers, upper-arm slimming, and cheek implants. Whatever was offered, no matter how extreme, it was necessary to be a new her. Her breasts were done and then redone. Her nipples thrice until perfect, and even her knees were dimpled, though she had trouble bending ever since, but, as she often said, "To whom do I have to curtsy anyway?"

Then it happened. The day she completely lost it—that struggle to be something other. It was July 17 at 2:27 p.m. at Barneys. You might wish to note that. (Third floor. Designer jeans. The saleslady was Pluckett. She had used her before.)

This is what transpired: She was looking in the three-way mirror, clearly squeezing into size eight jeans that she believed were mismarked. Pluckett agreed readily. "They were cut small— lots of Japanese shoppers, the yen being so strong." Pluckett apologized for the tight fit and brought forth another rack of size eights. Some French, some English, and even one pair made in the United States—imagine that?

"They were all to be eights," she said definitively to Pluckett. She wanted them that way. And that way only.

Ironically, she had just returned from a corporate meeting where she had stood up (not easily, knees and all) and was applauded for her department's double-digit grosses. That was fine.

She took the applause for herself. But she refused, even though knowing the bloom was off her rose (she admitted to forty-nine), to personally enter that category—for she was a size eight, a single digit and that was that. Pluckett pushed and she pulled. She squeezed and Pluckett zipped. She even caught some stomach skin (imagine that after a tummy tuck) right near her belly button that instantly formed a blood blister. Her obsession with figure eight was becoming dangerous. She was skating on thin ice. She sobbed into Pluckett's arms, her blue contacts red-rimmed, her eyes full of tears, hyperventilating and gasping from stress and surrender. "I can't do it anymore. I can't make it."

"Let me bring in the tens," said Pluckett gently.

So, on that fateful day, this former size eight succumbed to a double digit. Not without hesitation, she announced to the three of her in the mirror's reflection that she had entered a new category. She began to lecture her selves. "I do not want Ginger's eyes; I do not want Margaret's knees; I do not want Corrine's ex-husband; I do not want Aretha's career; I do not want Peggy's fortune; and I do not want to be an eight. I am a ten. I am a ten," she said with a tear-drenched smile. "But ten is what eight used to be, right, Pluckett?"

And Pluckett agreed.

Imaginary/Real

She was known for her bravery.

*It was front-page news the day she fearlessly fished
a woman out of a car after a crash on the Major
Deegan.*

*Risking her own life, with cars buzzing by, she managed
to save the young woman who was trapped by the side of
the road in an overturned car.*

*She was also known to get too close to the lions'
cage at the Central Park Zoo and was pulled away by
a policeman who threatened her with arrest should she
again step over the guard rail.*

*"That lion could eat you for breakfast," he said. And
she smiled calmly.*

---

*She even called home during the chaos of the big
Los Angeles earthquake of 1994. She survived it with
equanimity.*

*She was cool as a cucumber. (Why do we say
cucumbers are cool?)*

*She even put lipstick on before descending the
shaky hotel fire escape and collected extra slippers for*

those who had fled the quake barefoot and were quite hysterical.

———————

But in spite of her seeming fearlessness she had very specific imagined fears.

They surprised her in their simplicity when she compared them to life's true dangers.

How to explain this?

What made her terrified?

Whatever the cause, she was traumatized and frozen by an elevator door that closed.

This enclosure sent shivers through her, for she feared she would be locked in forever and no one would ever find her.

If she got stuck in an elevator in the summer, she worried she would die from heat exhaustion in this odious entrapment.

And in the winter, she feared she would freeze to death.

Unreasonable, yes—but paralyzing as well.

She was known to walk up, and later down, the thirty-seven flights to her office.

She would tell her workmates at the end of the day not to hold the elevator door for her, and she would later sneak down the stairs.

———————

She was also known to leave bathroom doors unlocked for fear of not being able to get out.

As a little girl she remembered asking her mother not to close the bedroom door. "Mommy, please leave the door open," she would say. "It scares me when it's closed."

She even wanted her closet open. "Please, Daddy, open the closet door."

And sometimes when no one was looking, before falling asleep, she would even open the drawers of her chests, giving freedom to the garments she believed were trapped inside.

And on cold nights she would tug open the window so the air outside would not be closed out.

———

There were other things.

Sometimes on a business trip, walls would walk.

The unfamiliarity of a given space would become a closet she was closeted in.

There were times when these moving walls would so scare her that she would have to go to the front desk and make idle chatter with a disinterested receptionist until the panic lifted.

Once in a hotel room at Cannes she felt suffocated by moving walls.

There were no return flights.

She explained to an airline attendant that her mother was gravely ill.

Obligingly, they found her a seat and she would be eternally grateful to the airline for saving her from a smothering and imaginary but real fear.

Oddly she was not afraid of flying, but the sound of the cabin door lowering and then catching would cause her to become violently dizzy and hyperventilate, losing breath—knowing she would die before takeoff.

———

Who was she?

She was smart, accomplished—a role model for many.

She was known as a Fortune 500 wunderkind.

And yet she was crippled by this closing-in, even though she knew it was all in her mind.

Her practical, common sense self knew that the elevator would land—and if it got stuck, so what?

She knew that the bathroom doors once locked would reopen.

She knew that walls could not walk.

She knew that when the plane landed the door would open and she would be able to disembark.

But that was her logical self.

———

What was it?

She asked a variety of well-trained shrinks of various disciplines from Freud to Jung.

Psychotherapists, behaviorists—fat, thin, wise, and twisted.

All agreed she suffered from claustrophobia, catastrophic thinking, and general anxiety.

The cause?

They blamed separately her cortisol levels, her genetics, a screwed-up fight-or-flight response, a post-traumatic experience, a displacement of a sexual nature . . .

She accepted all these causes but she needed a cure.

There was no way she could have any success with this detour.

Every job required a closed door of sorts.

Boardrooms, private confidential meetings, bathrooms where a locked door was a necessity.

But she would one day discover, through some mystery of chemistry, that her chemistry could be altered by a pill.

A pill that would in minutes allow doors to be closed,

Elevators to rise, and walls to stay put.

For this panic disorder, there was no reasoning that would accomplish what this tiny benzodiazepine pill, colloquially known as a benzo, could.

It became her dearest friend for life—the day she was prescribed a benzo by Dr. Woozoo.

Her friend Lucille warned her that she would become an addict. But yet she never did. Dependent, yes. Addicted, no.

How did this little pill, sometimes named Ativan, sometimes named Valium, Xanax, sometimes named Klonopin, open all doors for her?

Who knew?

But she now fearlessly rode to the top floors of the highest buildings.

She peered from the top of the Eiffel Tower and looked down from the observation deck of the Empire State Building—both requiring express elevators to the very highest point.

She locked every bathroom door and even read the entire paper while seated there.

Her business trips were never interrupted by walls closing in.

Her windows were open or closed depending on the weather.

Her closet doors were shut to keep out moths.

Wherever she was when she took the pill, she knew she would always be able to get out.

And then friends told her of their fears as she told them of hers.

One had a fear of heights,

Another, a fear of pigeons,

One a fear of tunnels,

Another of bridges,

And another, of airplanes—unable to fly.

And the oddest, a friend, Isaac, whose mother would scream at two words—zipper and purple.

"Be careful when you meet my mother," Isaac said, "not to say those two words."

Imagine that, *she thought.*

She began to think that though these terrors were illogical in the real world, they were meaningful in their owners' minds.

If a pill could stop all these fears, maybe a benzo was like insulin to a diabetic or penicillin to strep.

And so she lived her successful life clutching her pill case.

Knowing that normalcy was just a swallow away.

Waiting for the benzo to kick in so she could play the "I'm all right" game—and win.

She never abused them as Lucille had warned her.

She never forgot them though, always making sure this crutch was nearby.

And then one sad day her friend Lucille succumbed to a stroke at the age of forty-two

Just as Lucille's father had thirty years earlier.

At the funeral parlor, Lucille's coffin was open.

She was dressed beautifully and looked alive, like the friend she had been yesterday.

And when the funeral director lowered the cover of the coffin,

It clicked—forever.

True to old form, she felt faint and her head swirled,

So she quickly swallowed an Ativan,

Which took a short time to kick in.

And when it did,

She stood by Lucille's closed coffin fearlessly and delivered a beautiful elegy,

Bemoaning her great loss and praising Lucille's soul.

Lucille was at last boxed in forever.

This enclosure was not treatable.

But whatever its cause, her anxiety was treatable.

"Thank you, benzos," she said to herself. "My anti-terror pill,

And my little secret."

What's in a Name?

What's in a name?
So what if I don't remember his or yours?
What's it to you?
I refuse to panic!
But I do.

A senior moment?
Fuck that.
I pretend I don't care to remember, though I search
  with desperation.
Whozawhatchamacallit are you?
Am I losing it?
Am I denying serious forgetfulness?
Could this be a critical future sign of decay?
Or am I forgetting this "him" because there are more
  important things to remember?
Like my dog, Bogie.
I never forget him or Casablanca
Or Humphrey or Lauren
Because they have a permanent place in my heart.

You anonymous man at this party,
I know what you do.
You're in my business. You work in television.
I even know what I think of your work.
So, I'll pretend I know your name with this game:
ME: "Hi, hey, how's work going?"
HE: "Great. You look great."
ME: "Thanks. Fabulous tie. Who's the designer?"
HE: "Gucci."
ME: "Expensive! Ha, you must be doing well."
HE: "My wife bought it."

———————

He's married. Hmm. Who is he?
Ha, I laughed again,
And we laughed together—old friends,
One nameless.

———————

As a matter of fact, in my silent thoughts, I
   imagined this known unknown stranger's
   name was often subject to debate during his
   gestation.
His mother said, "I like the name Roger," and his
   father said, "Never."
And then his father said, "Peter," after his dead
   stepfather,
And his mother said, "Alex," after her grandfather who
   was blood and was a reputed violin maker.
And his father said, "Never ever!"

So what's in a name?
These parents came up with this unknown-er's name
    obviously as a compromise.
I like definition.
I like winners.
So what's the big deal?
In the first place, his name was of uncertain and
    debatable origin.

———————

What's in a name?
A name by any other name would smell as sweet.
Thank you, Shakespeare.
See, I remember his name.

———————

Memories come back.
I saw him at the opening of the documentary Gorilla.
We talked about how manipulated the film was.
We guessed it was not an Oscar contender.
"But you never know with that group," I said.
We were both members, I suppose.
What the hell is his name anyway?

———————

We said we must have lunch and I said I'd like that.
I said I'd call him.
Call who?
Doesn't matter.

And then as he drifted away
And I crossed this party floor,
Suddenly a thunderous brain synapse
Fought its way through.
Connection refreshed.
The name "Chris" appeared as if in a theater bijoux,
*   the last name Whea . . .*
Ah, yes, ah, yes. Mystery man was Chris Wheatley.
Chris Wheatley. Ah, there it is.
I never was a great fan of your work anyway, Chris
*   Wheatley.*
You're a nice guy though.

———————

So there it was . . .
And did it really matter that I remembered or not?

———————

A name by any other name would be as forgettable.

———————

Just fine forgetting, and for no reason wearying my
*   wracked frontal lobe for a torturous recall.*
Rushing to Sara across the room.
I know her well and her name without searching.
Always
Proof of instant recall.
"Sara, Sara,
Let's get out of here. So
Stifling.
I can't hear a thing

Or anything else."
So we did leave.
It was important to get fresh air.
And this I remember:

I remember leaving.

A Man with a Scythe
Rang My Doorbell

A man with a scythe rang my doorbell.
I saw him through the peephole.
I said he had the wrong apartment.
He said he wanted me.
I told him to go away.
He laughed and left.

————————

I called downstairs.
We had tight security.
The rents were high enough to offer better protection.
Neither the concierge nor the doorman had seen
    anyone.
I called a twenty-four-hour locksmith.
Expensive but worth it.
He came and installed a new lock.

The next night,
The man with the scythe returned
With the same scythe and a hood.
At least it looked like the same scythe.
I screamed for him to go away.
"Please, leave me alone," I begged.
I had just remodeled my kitchen and was not about to
   move to safer quarters.
I called downstairs.
"The hooded scythe-man is back!" I cried out.
Again, they had seen nothing.

———————

I called the locksmith.
The twenty-four-hour one.
He knew me now.
He came, installed another, stronger lock—a police lock.
More expensive but absolutely worth it.

———————

The next night,
You got it.
The hooded man with the scythe came back.
At least it looked like the same hood.
I saw his face through the keyhole.
It was a young boy's face.
I was less afraid. I asked him to please go away.
He said he wanted to be my friend.
That he knew a lot of people I knew.
I told him I had all the friends I needed.
And then he left.

I think he was hurt.
He said he'd be back.

———————

You know the drill.
I called the locksmith,
The twenty-four-hour one.
I woke him.
He had no more locks to offer.
"Crooks like the Grim Reaper," he said, "can get
*   through any lock and you have the best."*
I knew he was telling me the truth.

———————

Oddly, the man with the boy's face and the hood and
*   the scythe has not yet returned.*
But I know he'll be back.

And maybe, just maybe, I'll be ready for him.
Maybe my time will have come.
Maybe life will hurt too badly.
And anyway, he said he knew some of the people I
*   knew.*
And I miss them.

+1.75: An Insight

ONE DAY, some thirty years ago, I suddenly could not see a telephone number in a Manhattan phone book. From that day forth, I was not ready for my close-up. No matter how many dime-store pairs of glasses I've bought lo these many years, hardly a day goes by when I can find any of these reading glasses anywhere. I've done everything—hung them around my neck, placed them in various places at home and in the office. I've even put them in raincoats and bathrobe pockets. And, yet, whenever I need a pair, they're nowhere to be found. I have hundreds of them. So, I pay the wrong total on the Chinese takeout, miss a key word in an article, or often order the wrong salad from an eyeglass-less read of a dinner menu.

Oh, cruel fate! Yet, this continual search for definition led me to ponder if possibly this seismographic vision change coincided with the cataclysms of menopause, empty nests, and the necessity of sensible shoes. Was this blurring a concealed inspirational message from Above? A silent nudge for me to start to observe differently, to see the world from a different frame of being—a reminder of the forest for the trees? For all my lived life, so far, I had intended to focus on, obsess on, little things. They meant a lot. They often kept me off track, like a train halting for a small pebble. I was impeded by an odd offhanded remark, a slightly different color hair-dye job, an inconsistency in a movie's continuity. Detail, details, detailing.

And so I thought to take wisdom from this clear lack of clarity and accept it and try to take it in stride. "See the big picture," I said. Create a mantra that says, "I will not be forced off track or piqued by the little things—these tiny bugs that seem so big, that I allow to screw up the mechanism of my daily enjoyment of life."

On an ugly hair day, with a creased face returning home from the L.A. red-eye and smelling of jet fuel, my husband (also vision deprived) opened the apartment door and said, unrehearsed, how beautiful I was—once and now. Honest—he said that.

Suddenly, I understood the compensatory power of a diminishing close-up. The glory of the loss of acuity that I thought I had missed. I ohmmed to myself an appreciation for the philosophical and psychological advantages of seeing life from a distance. The forest. The whole picture.

So on a cloudless night, I took off my +1.75 crutches to observe the clarity of what was far away. The moon, the stars, and the sky—all so beautiful and clear. My Universe. The Universe.

Gliding Gracefully
into Gravity

A SIZE TWO walks by with the right answer to a film we are working on. She is beautiful. She is young. She gets it right. "Terrific," you say. It is not her fault that she is perfect and smart and half your age.

And the bronchitis lingers. You caught it from her. She whipped it in a week. You're onto a thousand coughs and a thousand sleepless nights. She didn't mean to have a great immune system.

Philip Roth depresses you. Does he have to be so brilliant about exits and ghosts? Why does Zuckerman have to be an aging curmudgeon and incontinent while forgetting to change his urine-stinking diaper? Any one of these signs of decay would have been enough.

And how about the woman who grabbed you on the Saks escalator? You didn't need an outfit anyway.

"Sheila, Sheila. Sheila Nevins. Remember me? Audrey Melznik, we graduated the same year from Barnard."

"Oh, yes, Audrey. Of course, I remember you." (I don't.) Children? Yes. Grandchildren? Five. Wow. All boys? Great. Harvard? Great. Oh, sorry. Two husbands. One dead. Oh, sorry. Life. Gottagogottago.

Audrey Melznik is old. She is my age. Her hair is gray. She is plumpish. She let herself be old. I hate her. Or do I respect her? What the fuck am I so upset about? Damn it. Who needs Audrey Melznik anyway?

Is it the twenty extra pounds I gained since college that've got me in a tizzy? The high-heeled shoes that now hurt? Didn't used to. Is it the affair I do/don't want and, anyway, it's too late. Is it the look on a baby colleague's face when I draw a blank on a name or don't know the band called something-or-other? "Oh, yes. I think I've heard of them." Liar. What is it that panics me so?

I think it's death. Not probably. Death. And age. Why can't I face aging with grace? Does anyone ever whistle anymore? I want to meet Mother Time with a pas de deux. A curtsy for the scythe. A refined readiness. That's all. Is all. Why, oh, why can't I . . .

I want to celebrate the longevity of my life. My mom never made it. My dad gave it to cigarettes. Why am I hiding? I am a product of magazine covers that screech: "Young at any price. Buy me!" The saleslady who says the ill-fitting clothes look great on me and make me look young—Sold! To me, the fool who buys the spiel. Please, God, I'm an atheist who wants to look young. I have enough Botox in me to detonate Iran.

Why can't I go gracefully into gravity? This aging terror. Why can't I bellow on Times Square to the disinterested passersby, "Sixty, seventy, eighty, ninety, one hundred . . . and counting." Say it. Say it loud. Who am I fooling really? The health plan told the doctor and he knows. The dentist sees my teeth and he knows. And Google told Wikipedia. What's the big secret?

The secret is I don't want to say good-bye. I don't think it's fair to have worked so hard and given up so much time to not have more time.

If they can make a car without a driver, why can't they make a me that goes on?

So that's the secret. I'm angry that it's almost over, just when I understand I've just begun.

The Wrong Kind of Hot

CHOCK FULL o'Nuts was an old-time coffee shop with great raisin cream cheese sandwiches and coffee that was always the right kind of hot. Hardly the place for a game changer. And yet it happened to be one.

My mother was born with an awful disease called Raynaud's phenomenon. Most of the time, Raynaud's simply means you have a lack of circulation in your extremities. Annoying, yes, but nothing to be alarmed about. But my mom had a severe case, the kind where your fingers, toes, and then even arms and legs would lose circulation and go from blue to black and then become gangrenous. It's incredibly painful. If they turn black, they never heal and then they die. And the only treatment is amputation.

I grew up fearful of decay. A black nail meant a finger above the knuckle was in danger and eventually would lead to an amputation. My mother's disease started ruthlessly with her fingers—first it was the second fingertip on her left hand, and then, over the years, it progressed.

Mount Sinai Hospital in New York was my second home. I knew all the nurses. I knew exactly how much change was needed in every vending machine. I wanted sweet things. Life was sour. Yet no Raisinets, no Jujubes, no Almond Joy could take away the bitter taste of life's brutal entrance fee.

"Mom," I would say, "why do we live if we have to suffer?"

And my mom would say, "What's the choice?"

And so it would be that I grew up sad and terrified, thinking every cold was terminal pneumonia, every small paper cut a future amputation. After all, I was my mother's daughter.

My mother was hard on me. I never seemed to do anything right. Pain disturbed any pleasure she might have had. Every event was fraught with the need for pain medication and my nursing skills. If I resisted this servitude, I would be blamed. She told me again and again that I was selfish. We didn't have money for help. My mother was sure angry living in Hell, and I was her closest driver in this River Styx. Sure, I had a sister, but she was seven and a half years younger. So, of course, I was her caretaker too. Sheila, do this; Sheila, do that. Sheila, you didn't do this; Sheila, you didn't do that.

I loved my mother but at the same time resented her. While my friends' mothers shopped and worried about the color of their hair as it turned gray and their Fire and Ice matching lipstick and nail color, I lived in a private war-torn universe. I lived with a noose around my neck. And so I became . . . me.

My father was never home. He worked at the post office, booked bets for the mailmen, and spent his nights playing cards in what were known then as goulash joints on the Lower East Side of Manhattan. These were working middle-class clubs where men would play poker for cash and bet on horses and sporting events. They all smoked. My father smoked three packs a day. His nickname was Benny P.O. "*Hey, Benny, I want to bet on the Knicks game. What are the odds? Who's the favorite?*"

One day when I was a sophomore living in a Barnard dorm, commuting home frequently at my mother's beck and call, my mom came uptown for lunch. She was driving a newly equipped car with odd hand brakes that could be maneuvered with her elbow. She was proud of its adaptability, and she zoomed city-wide thanks to the Rusk Institute, the post office's medical plan, and Volvo mechanics. By this time, she had suffered an amputation of her left arm just below her elbow. As ugly as the amputation was, it was a great improvement over the creeping crud of gangrene and the excruciating pain of a dying limb.

In 1960, my mom was only in her early forties. This seemed old to me then. I was born when she was twenty-two. She had come that day for lunch, wanting to go to Chock full o'Nuts to get one of their famous raisin cream cheese sandwiches and the always just-right hot coffee. She seemed happy for once to see me, happy to be mobile and driving by herself, happy to be ambulatory though amputated.

It was a sultry, too warm day in May. Her pleated dress had long sleeves, the one on the right arm rolled up and the one on the left tied in a knot below the stump. (There must be a better word for stump but frankly, why euphemize the ugly?)

The air-conditioning in the restaurant was off. It was tolerable but Mom was hot with the knotted sleeve. That amputated arm had ghostlike sweat that would often roll down and wet the inside, as if the stump was crying and trapped without air.

Mom said her arm was stifling, stifling. I rolled up her left sleeve, untying the knot. I unbuttoned the second button of her dress and fanned her with my study notepad.

"Any better?" I asked.

"Not really," she said.

Our sandwiches came, and the perfect coffee. Hot on a hot day, but perfectly so. Mom rested her stump on the counter. Her shortened arm was heavy to lift and too short to hide below the counter.

Suddenly from the other side of the S-shaped counter, a middle-aged woman with a kinky permed bob and harlequin glasses, who was fanning herself with a newspaper, yelled out. "Please, ladies, I'm eating. It is rude to expose that arm. It makes me want to throw up."

That's what she said. And that's what I remember she said. And every time we'd tell this story to close friends, or sympathetic physical therapy folk, or just to each other, that's what my mom remembered too.

I apologized to this bitch, which was odd for me. I wasn't the apologetic type. I was afraid to catch this woman's eye. I was afraid she would hurt me or make a bigger scene. Everybody in the restaurant listened. I rolled the sleeve down and retied the knot. "Sorry, sorry," I said to her. I was embarrassed.

Everything was going too fast. Customers started taking sides. The woman to our left said that the lady who spoke out was a crazy lady and she was disgusting. And yet a man on our right said that, after all, this is a place to eat and some things are not meant to be seen while eating. The two squabbled, these strangers.

Mom and I hurriedly left the restaurant. The sandwiches were never going to be tasty again. The coffee was never going to be the right kind of hot. All was cold.

I cried in the fixed-up car. Mom said the woman was nasty, maybe a little crazy too. But I cried because I had not yelled back. I should have said, "Fuck you! This is my mom. She has a horrible, horrible disease that you are lucky enough not to have."

I was furious that I had apologized. Why had I? Why was I ashamed? Why was I a beggar and not a victor? Why had I let this woman seize this moment? Why?

People talk of moments that make you change. That determine who you are. This moment was mine. I would realize that I understood people and their suffering, and somewhere, in defending their difference, was a place for me. I had failed once and I wouldn't fail again.

So I would grow to champion stories about those less fortunate. Stories of real people. Mostly I chose to tell stories of the struggle to triumph in an uncertain and often cruel world.

I've always been interested in those who need visibility, notoriety, and acceptance—anonymous victims of unfairness, deprivation, and poverty. I guess I was determined to right my ineffectiveness at that lunch-counter visit so long ago. Documentaries talked back while I had been unable. They speak without shyness—no apologizing. Blatant truth. Ugly at times, yet always true.

Two leftover cups of coffee and raisin bread with cream cheese had lost their taste forever.

Chock full o'Nuts.

The wrong kind of hot.

To Fur or Not to Fur:
Eden's Dilemma

S HE HAD always wanted a fur coat—fox or mink or beaver, mouton or Persian lamb. She had always *cruelly* wanted one, though she was a bleeding-heart liberal about everything else. But this "fur-mania" went back . . . way, way back.

Eden had been born poor. Daddy was a postman. Mommy ran a laundromat. Laundromats were for people who couldn't afford washing machines. You get the spin. But Eden was determined to break the cycle. She wanted more.

Eden went to a *fancy girl*'s school, and not because she was rich, obviously, but because she was smart—smarter than her *fancy girl* classmates. She was the poor little scholarship kid, the one with the best grades.

Mostly, Eden did not suffer from self-esteem issues. She knew that she had what it took. But one day, every year, was an exception—Parent/Teacher Day. This day was always fraught for Eden, because the other mothers came decked out, but Eden's mother, Ellen Rosedale, had nothing to wear but laundromat items. And so, in preparation, Mrs. Rosedale's friend, Sophie Sonnenberg, would lend Ellen her clothes to make a good impression. Mrs. Sonnenberg lent Eden's mother her diamond earrings, her alligator bag, her suede high heels, and most importantly, her big fox-fur coat. Sophie Sonnenberg, you see, had a great saleslady job at Macy's and got closeout items at a steal.

Eden was proud of her mother's visual presentation, and Mrs. Ellen Rosedale beamed at the academic acclaim her daughter always earned. As soon as mother and daughter would leave the school building, however, Mrs. Rosedale would immediately take off the agonizing heels and change into her Hush Puppies, and she and Eden would rush to catch the bus home, where Sophie Sonnenberg always waited anxiously for her items to be returned. Mrs. Sonnenberg would say, dusting off her returned clothes and shaking her fox fur, "Eden, you are smarter than all those rich girls, and brains are worth all the money in the world!"

Now, when Eden grew up, she became a very successful lawyer and litigator. She graduated from the best college and law school, was on law review, and was first in passing the difficult July New York bar exam. In these areas she always excelled, but life had not been completely fair to her. Her father, the postman, left her mother at forty-five for a twenty-four-year-old postal clerk whom he had met while studying for a zip code exam. And her mother, at fifty-eight, slipped on a soapy floor in her laundromat and never fully recovered. Eden provided her mother with the best 'round-the-clock nurses, who took excellent care of Mrs. Rosedale. They called her Ellen, many having known her from the laundromat—since, being nurses, few had the money to own their own washer/dryer. But Mrs. Rosedale died in her sleep at age sixty, leaving a hefty sum of medical bills, which her brokenhearted daughter could now well afford to pay.

There are certain things that poor girls want when they are no longer poor. One is a good dentist, and the other, especially in Eden's case, is a fur coat. What she spent on her teeth she could keep to herself, but ever since those days when her mother had been forced to borrow Sophie Sonnenberg's fox fur, Eden dreamt of a fur coat of her own. This mania was a secret passion she kept to herself, an obsession. However, in the PC world in which she lived, making this fantasy a reality was verboten. Her friends were peaceniks, environmentalists, legal-aid lawyers, and animal rights activists—all for whom fur coats were out! They were operatic in condemnation of "those bitches who wear fur!" Once, at her law firm, the oldest partner's wife dared to wear a sweater with a fur collar. This enraged Myra, one of her favorite paralegals, who was even an admitted right-wing Republican.

I've worked so hard, thought Eden, *lost my mother to a soap sud, never speak to my father anymore, don't have a steady guy-friend. What do I have? A big fat paycheck, and I can't even have a fur coat!*

Eden could be seen wandering furtively around the fur salons of various department stores, caressing coats she could never have: the beaver, the mink, the raccoon, the seal. Each filled her with unspeakable longing and personal disgust. Once she actually tried one on. She felt extremely beautiful and despicably carnivorous simultaneously. Eden fled the store, dreaming of owning a coat, and hating herself for it.

On January 23, 2016, a blizzard descended on New York. It happened to be a big day at Eden's law firm: bonus day, and hers was huge. She had earned it having won a case that required the slyness of a fox and the speed of a coyote. Slip-sliding home, check in her bag, she passed Lord & Taylor. In the window was a mean, warm mannequin dressed in a slithery mink, with a sign beneath that read:

BEN KAHN FURS
30% off

Eden walked into the store. She was on autopilot. She escalated to the third floor and made a sharp turn directly into the Kahn boutique. Her heart was pounding. The hunt was on. *I will, I need, I can,* and something told her she would.

It was beautiful. It was mink and long with a stand-up collar. She looked and felt like a million dollars in it. She had almost earned that much. And so she bought it quickly. $4,312.64 with 30 percent off. She was a selfish, vainglorious superficial—but she loved that coat. She told the saleslady she felt awful wearing an animal's skin. "Forget it, baby," the saleslady explained. "They raise 'em for this very reason."

What does that mean? Eden thought. It only made her feel worse.

When she got home, she told no one. For the rest of the winter months, she wore her mink around the house, like a bathrobe. Once she slunk to the grocery store to buy some milk and coffee but quickly rushed back, pulling the animal skin up around her face so as to not be seen. One night her building's heat went off and she slept warmly, lovingly, beautifully with the beast that she had slaughtered. *How cruel am I?* she thought that morning as she put her fur away and donned her cloth coat for another chilly walk to work. *I am hateful!*

And winter became spring and spring became summer and Eden kept her fur a secret. When winter came again, a bad snowstorm kept everyone home from work. So, Eden slipped into a local movie theatre wearing her secret fur. The movie was *March of the Penguins*. Eden felt criminal, dirty, and hurried home. She hated the movie. Anthropomorphizing penguins—now, really! Granted, the movie was over the top, but Eden still felt like a serial killer.

Christmas is a time of giving. Carl, one of the divorced partners at Eden's firm, was spending more and more time in her bed. She liked it. He was hot and loving. Her secret was tucked away in her closet, and once, after a few drinks, she almost showed it to him, but she was afraid he'd leave her. After all, he'd waited a year for his red hybrid and was thoroughly obsessed with miles per gallon. As things were, Carl really liked Eden, and she had decided not to test him. He toasted her naked imperfect body with champagne. He found her perfect. But would he like her furried? She wasn't confident enough to find out.

On the corner of the apartment building in which Eden lived was a wonderful thrift shop called Helping Hands. Eden had given them expensive sweaters, shirts, and shoes when she grew tired of them. The volunteers were always ultra-kind and thanked her profusely, giving her substantial tax deductions as well. Whenever Eden would drop a package off, their parting words were always, "God bless you." Eden liked that, because inside she knew she was evil.

Time passed, and the pressure was mounting. Carl's suits were moving into her closet, and Eden feared that the coat would be outed. One night she even dreamt the coat left her apartment on all fours, eating the M&M's on her coffee table and breaking her expensive crystal vase. She awoke trembling, fearful, resolved. The dream had pushed her. She knew what she had to do.

She rolled up the coat in a Safeway shopping bag; on her way to work, she would drop it off at Helping Hands. She rushed out. Helping Hands was closed, but in the window was one of their volunteers setting up Christmas lights as window trim. Eden rapped on the door. The kindly, God-fearing lady opened it. "Please," said Eden, "take this. It's a coat. Fur. A gift. It's worth thousands. I don't need a receipt. Just give it away."

"God bless you, my dear one," said the volunteer.

"And you too," said Eden. Free at last. Eden was free at last. She had finally disposed of her burden.

Several days later, Eden and Carl, hand in hand, passed Helping Hands. In the window was Eden's beautiful coat. Her heart warmed. Her eyes sparkled. "Do I deserve that?" Eden coquettishly asked Carl.

CARL: You deserve the world.
EDEN: Pretty, isn't it?
CARL: Want it?
EDEN: But, it's fur.

CARL: But you'd be giving money to the poor. You didn't
      kill the animal. Is it mink?

EDEN: I guess?

CARL: You deserve it.

EDEN: But it's killing!

CARL: It's already dead. It will keep you warm. Eden,
      please, let me buy it for you.

EDEN: Oh, Carl . . .

CARL: Please.

EDEN: Oh, Carl.

CARL: I love you. I'd love for you to have it.

EDEN: Really?

CARL: Really!

And so the loving couple went into Helping Hands. The woman who showed them the coat was the same volunteer who had been decorating the window several days before. Eden raised a finger to her lips. *Shhhh* . . . It was their little secret. The ticket price was two thousand dollars. Carl wanted her to have it.

"Please, Eden. Let me get it for you." She tried it on and it fit . . . miraculously.

"Oh, Carl," she said, "are you really sure? An animal died for me."

"You didn't kill it, Eden. Like I said, it was dead already . . . and I'm dying of love." Eden giggled with glee, though she was not the giggling type. Christmas cheer. The volunteers put the coat in a Safeway shopping bag, tied with a green-and-red ribbon. Carl charged it and got two-thousand-plus airline miles. Eden told Carl it was the best Christmas gift she'd ever received. After all, it was secondhand, somebody else's selfish desire. *They* had helped feed the poor and clothe the hungry. Or was it clothe the poor and feed the hungry? Most importantly, Carl really cared for her.

I can wear this without feeling guilt, Eden thought. *I mean, really. We eat meat, we wear leather, and I'm a secondhand rose.*

"God bless you," said the volunteer. "God bless you both."

And so Eden kept the coat that Carl gave her. It was her little secret and her childhood revenge. And as life would go on, she would marry Carl and never, despite both their economic success, ever buy another fur. But, there are some things you have to do because your childhood tells you to. Eden forgave herself, and that very day she read in the paper that a tiger had eaten a man at the San Francisco Zoo, and somehow she felt exonerated. But as a top-notch lawyer, she hoped that a jury would find her innocent.

The Art of Book Signing

I swore I would never sign my first book.
It seemed degrading to hawk "sales by signature."
And, anyway, my signature would mean nothing:
This book was definitely my only one, and I was never going to
    write another.
And that was that.

My first book signing required a signature. But I refused to sign.
I simply disappeared after the presentation.
But then came more official encounters,
where I was told that book signings were obligatory and that I
    had no choice.
I simply must sign.

The people wanted signatures.
But why? I wasn't a star. The book was worth nothing more on
    eBay. And I was a lefty with a bizarre signature. Anyway, I was
    not dying just yet, and even if I was, my signature would be of
    no value in my aftermath. But this reading public wanted it.
    Bizarre but true. My small and tidy public wanted my script.

And so I learned the art of the obliging sign-off—a fine skill I had
    never cultivated before.

In the beginning, the books I signed had insincere messages like "Always best," "Thanks for buying my book," "Good luck," "xoxo Sheila." The signature I wrote looked crooked, and the expressions were duplicative and meaningless.

And so, in my search to make this life meaningful, I turned to the art of documentary, my chosen craft, and began to ask questions of the reader.

Who were they?

Why did they read or want to read my book?

What made them interested?

And then this world of signage began to have a charm of its own.

Some highlights:

> Your name, I asked.
> *Belle.*
> Lovely name. Is this book for you?
> *No, it's for my daughter.*
> What's her name?
> *Sherrie.*
> Oh. A gift?
> *Well, yes. Sherrie's not well.*
> I'm so sorry.
> *She's at Sloan Kettering, and she's in the last of Stage 4 endometrial cancer.*
> Oh dear. I'm so sad for you. Will she have time?
> *Excuse me?*
> Will she have time to read this silly book of mine?
> *I'll read her just the funny parts. It is funny. And it will make her laugh.*
> Oh, ok. That makes me feel good. What will you do about the sad parts?
> *I won't read her those.*
> Good idea.

And this is what I wrote for Belle:

> Dear Sherrie,
> Your mother loves you so very much. More than the sun
> and the moon and the stars all together. And she would
> bring them all to you if she possibly could.

And then I asked Belle,
Should I add an "o" to "loves you so"?
If you'd like.
Like "your Mother loves you s-o-o-o much"? I added two
    o's. She smiled.
She'll like that. Thanks.
No, thank you. Good luck. God's love.
Thank you, Sheila.

That encounter was one of many.
Suddenly I began to like signing.
I asked questions.
And, mostly, the people answered.
The answers were frivolous often, giggled, or impactful, tearful,
    questioning. I had friends for this very moment, brought on
    by left-handed clumsy penmanship.

Another example:

I have a son who has Tourette's.
It's tough. Did you like my story about it? My son had
    Tourette's, too.
Very much.
Did it help you?
No, not really.
I'm sorry.
Nothing to be sorry about. My son's still at home.
Oh dear.

Your kid in the book got better.
Yes, that's true.
My son got worse.
I'm so sorry. So my signature, who is it for?
For me.
Oh.
Why not? She laughed. *It's the same price. Signing is free.*
Yes. *I smiled. And we both laughed.*
Anyway, she said. *I heard you write about husbands screwing
    your best friends.*
Well those are just a few stories.
I really need to read those.
I hope they don't disappoint you.
I can take it, she said. *Remember, my son has a bad case of
    Tourette's.*
That's true. Sorry about your boy. What's your name?
Annie.
Ok.

And I wrote,

> Dear Annie,
> Enjoy this book. I'm sorry you have to deal with Tourette's,
> and I applaud you questioning life's turns and often pain-
> ful nuances.

She read the inscription. *Thank you, Sheila.*
No, thank you, Annie. Good luck with your boy.
He's forty-five now.
Oh, well good luck anyway. They're always kids to us.
True. Thanks.

And so it would go.
Confessions, questions, intimacies—shared for the moment until
    the ink dried. I used an ink pen.

And then the guy with the suspenders and the stained shirt . . .

> To whom is this for? For you? *Few of my readers had been men.*
> *It's for my mother.*
> Ah, how thoughtful. For Mother's Day?
> *Well, yes and no.*
> No? For who then?
> *Well my mother's dead.*
> Oh. Will you see her shortly?
> *Oh no. I'm not into that crap.*
> Oh, I see.
> *No afterlife shit for me. But reincarnation—that's for sure. We both loved cats, my mom and me. I have three. Two were hers.*
> Oh. Cats are lovely.
> *My mother's dead, but I collect things she would like, for when she comes back. When we come back. It's a shrine for the future.*
> Ah, yes. Will you come back as cats?
> *We won't know for sure until it actually happens.*
> Of course. How foolish of me. What should I say to your mom?
> *Whatever you think.*
> Well, what was, is, her name?
> *Vera.*

And I wrote,

> To Vera,
> Your son loves you beyond everyday love. The cats are well and miss you. To the future, whatever.

Perfect, he said. *She'll like that.*
Oh good. Give her my best when you see her as whatever.

Whatever. And thanks, Miss.

But the one that stands out with a real afterlife is the one from Great Barrington.

Hello. Thanks for buying my book.
I already read it from the Barrington Public Library.
Oh, well is this copy for a friend?
No, just for me. And I wanted to ask you a favor.
Sure.
You know the story about separate beds?
Yes.
Well Sam, my husband, and I have been married for forty years.
Congratulations.
When I broach the subject of me taking my son Jacob's room and us having separate bedrooms, Sam dismisses it. I think he's afraid of how it would look to other people.
Well it's quite common after long marriages. *I said this without any backup material—my story based on peeks into the bedrooms of the seasoned-married.* How can I help? I'm not like a marriage counselor.
I know. But if I buy the book, could you write a note to Sam? He likes your work on television. On HBO. He's a fan of Real Sex.
Well I don't really work there anymore, and you don't have to buy the book. I can just send him a note.
Yeah, but you make it official in a hardcover. Could you write him a note in the book?
Sure.

Dear Sam,
Thanks for liking the *Real Sex* shows. You might especially like the story of married people having separate

bedrooms that's in my book. It doesn't mean no sex or
no love.
Just read my story.
Your wife is beautiful. Your wife is great.
xoxo Sheila

And Sam's wife said, *Thank you.*

I had written a note. My book was, for her, just a blank pad
Made legitimate by a hard cover.
Pricey, instructional. But then why not?
I signed her book with a smile.

Trust me, it wasn't a long line that was waiting.
I now signed gleefully. I questioned the purchaser.
Me—a Dr. Ruth, a Dr. Phil, a first-time author with a pen.
And why not?
For sorrow and smiles, con-fucking-fessions and surprises,
Signing—I go forth.

"Next in line," I said.

Acknowledgments

I couldn't and wouldn't have tried this experiment without the sharp wit and persistence of Joni Evans. I would like to thank Mel Berger for his confidence and Larry Kramer for his magical inspiration. Thank you Susan Benaroya for being someone I can always count on. And a very special thanks to the technological wizard Rob Forlenza.

I would never have had the patience to sit still if it weren't for Amy Einhorn and the lessons in obedience and insight from Stephanie Kelly, and I can't forget my drill sergeant, Chance Morrison.

And a special "Bravo!" to the readers of the audiobook: Cynthia Adler, Alan Alda, Bob Balaban, Christine Baranski, Kathy Bates, Ellen Burstyn, RuPaul Charles, Glenn Close, Katie Couric, John Henry Cox, Blythe Danner, Lena Dunham, Edie Falco, Tovah Feldshuh, Whoopi Goldberg, Gayle King, Diane Lane, Sandra Lee, Judith Light, Jenna Lyons, Audra McDonald, Janet Mock, Rosie O'Donnell, Jean Richards, Liz Smith, Lesley Stahl, Gloria Steinem, Martha Stewart, Meryl Streep, Marlo Thomas, Lily Tomlin, Gloria Vanderbilt, and Diane von Furstenberg.

I would now like to thank my personal alphabet, the people

who have inspired me more than they may know. Some of them are no longer here, but they're with me. Especially Carrie Fisher, who I will miss as long as I am able to miss.

A—Abbey Curran, Adam Birnbaum, Al Maysles, Al Perlmutter, Alan Raymond, Alex Gibney, Alexandra Pelosi, Alexandra Shiva, Alexandra Wolfe, Alexis Bloom, Amy Gray, Amy Rice, Amy Schatz, Anderson Cooper, Andrew Jarecki, Andrew Rossi, Andy Cohen, Andy Lack, Anna Wintour, Annie Sundberg, Anthony Bregman, Ari Emanuel, Ari Shavit, Arthur Cohn, Asheba Edghill, Atiyah Robinson, Audrey Gordon

B—Barbara Taylor Bradford, Barbara Caver, Barbara Kopple, Barbara Walters, Beatrice Sagar, Beth Levison, Bill Chase, Bill Guttentag, Bill Nelson, Billie Lourd, Billy DiMichele, Bingham Ray, Brandon Bonart, Brent Brolin, Brett Morgan, Brett Ratner, Brian Oakes, Brian Siberell, Brooks Barnes, Bruce Grivetti, Bruce Ratner, Bruce Sinofsky, Bryan Lourd

C—Camille Bernier-Green, Carol Bober, Caroline Bleeke, Carolyn Strauss, Casey Bloys, Catie Lazarus, Cecile Richards, Charlene Bitzas, Charles Cohen, Charlie Kafferman, Chris Albrecht, Chris Hegedus, Chris Moukarbel, Christine Vachon, Cindi Berger, Cindy Adams, Courteney Monroe, Cynthia McFadden

D—D. A. Pennebaker, Dan Birman, Dan Chaykin, Dan Cogan, Dan Klein, Dan Lehmann, Dan Osheyack, Dan Reed, Dan Setton, Dana Perry, Dr. Daniel Baker, Daniel Junge, Daphne Pinkerson, Daryl Roth, Dave Baldwin, Dave Bell, David Chase, David Furnish, David Magdahl, David Webster, Davyne Verstandig, Dawn Ostroff, Debora Spar, Delia Ephron, Dennis Hof, Diane Foley, Diane Sokolow, Diane Wyermann, Dick Parsons, Dolores Morris, Don Ganem, Don Hewitt, Don Mischer, Donna Archer, Donna Daniels, Donna Satow, Dorothy Rabinowitz, Doug Block, Doug McGrath, Drew Nieporent, Dyllan McGee

E—Eames Yates, Eamonn Bowles, Edward Mapplethorpe, Elaine Stritch, Elissa Schein, Ellen Futter, Ellen Goosenberg-

Kent, Ellen Krass, Ellen Levine, Ellen Frey McCourt, Elliot Thomson, Elvis Mitchell, Eric Kessler, Eric Landgraf, Erin Buckley, Erin Lee Carr, Esther Kartiganer, Ethel Kennedy, Eva Zeisel

F—Fareed Zakaria, Fay Ennis, Fenton Bailey, Fionn Campbell, Fisher Stevens, Fran Lebowitz, Francine du Plessix Gray, Francine LeFrak, Frank D'Amico, Frank Doelger, Frank Marshall, Frank Rich, Frazer Pennebaker, Fred Bimbler, Esq.

G—Gaby Monet, Gary Goetzman, Gary Springer, Geeta Gandbhir, Geof Bartz, George Kunhardt, George Schlatter, George Stevens, Gerda Klein, Gina Heyman, Gladys Murphy, Gordon Parks, Grace Hightower, Greg Barker, Greg Rhem, Griffin Dunne, Gwen Morrison

H—Hank Stuever, Sir Harold Evans, Harry Belafonte, Harvey Weinstein, Heidi Ewing, Heidi Fleiss, Helen Whitney, Henry Louis Gates Jr., Henry Schleiff, Hope Litoff, Howard Rosenman, Howard Shapiro

I—Irene Taylor Brodsky, Isaac Mizrahi

J—Jack Lechner, Jackie Glover, Jacob Bernstein, Jacques D'Amboise, James Lapine, James Marsh, James O'Shea, Jane Anderson, Dr. Jane Galasso, Jane Nelson, Jane Rosenthal, Jane Wagner, Jason Blum, Jason Shandell, Jay Roewe, Jean Doumanian, Jeff Bewkes, Jeff Klein, Jeffery Wright, Jeffrey Toobin, Jen Kelly, Jennifer Estess, Jenny Rivas, Jerry Weintraub, Jesse Weinraub, Jessica Driscoll, Jillian Laub, Jim Gandolfini, Jim McDonald, Jim McGreevey, Joan Juliet Buck, Joan Ganz Cooney, Joan Kron, Joana Vicente, Joanna Coles, Joanna Scholl, Joe Berlinger, John Battsek, John Canemaker, John Guare, John Hoffman, John Horan, Esq., John Murphy, John Sloss, Jon Alpert, Jonathan Demme, Jonathan Klein, Josh Braun, Josh Fox, Judit Ungar, Judy Twersky, Julia Reed, Julian Schlossberg, Julie Anderson, Julie Goldman, Julie Salamon, Juliet Weber

K—Karen Goodman, Kary Antholis, Kate Amend, Kate Davis, Katharina Otto-Bernstein, Katherine Oliver, Kathleen Hale, Kelly Sheehy, Ken Cobb, Kenneth Cole, Kevin Butler, Dr. Kevin Morrissey, Keri Putnam, Kristina Schake

L—Lana Iny, Larissa Bills, Larry Brilliant, Dr. Laura Fisher, Laura Poitras, Laurie Anderson, Laylah Mohammad, Len Amato, Lesli Klainberg, Lin Arison, Linda Kenney Baden, Linda Ellerbee, Linda Stasi, Lindsey Pearl, Lisa Hedley, Lisa Heller, Lisa Jackson, Lisa Garcia Quiroz, Lisanne Skylar, Liz Garbus, Liz Swados, Liza Burnett Fefferman, Lori Seid, Lou Ciesco, Dr. Louis Katz, Lucille Nieporent, Lucinda Desir, Lucy Jarvis, Lucy Walker, Lynn Grossman

M—Maciek Albrecht, Marc Levin, Marc Urman, Dr. Marcel Tuchman, Mary Willa Gummer, Mary Wells Lawrence, Mary Tyler Moore, Mary Wallace, Maria Cooper-Janis, Maria Cuomo-Cole, Maria Shriver, Maria Zuckerman, Marie Brenner, Marina Abramovic, Marina Zenovich, Mark D'Arcy, Mark Subias, Dr. Marlene Marko, Maro Chermayeff, Martha Nelson, Martin Garbus, Mathilde Bonnefoy, Matt Drudge, Matt O'Neill, Matt Shea, Maura Pesantez, Maureen Dowd, Max Lewkowicz, Megan Mylan, Megan O'Hara, Mel Stuart, Mette Hoffman Meyer, Meredith Estess, Michael Bacon, Michael Baden, Michael Barker, Michael Cohen, Michael Fuchs, Michael Lombardo, Michael Moore, Dr. Michele Green, Michelle Byrd, Mike Ryan, Mikki Lam, Miky Wolf, Mira Nair, Dr. Mitch Rosenthal, Mitchell Block, Morgan Spurlock, Mother Angele, Mother Dolores Hart, Dr. Myron Shapero

N—Nancy Abraham, Nancy Buirski, Nancy Geller, Nancy Josephson, Nancy Lefkowitz, Nancy Lesser, Nathaniel Kahn, Dr. Neal Schultz, Neil Genzlinger, Neil Leifer, Dr. Nelson Novick, Nick Doob, Nick Fraser, Nick Loxha, Nikki Bethel, Nina Davenport, Nina Rosenstein, Noah Thomson, Nola Safro, Nora Ephron, Dr. Nora Volkow, Norman Pearlstine, Dr. Norman Sussman

O—Oliver Stone, Oskar Eustis, Dr. Owen Lewis

P—Pamela Taylor, Pat Fili-Krushel, Patrick Goldstein, Patti Kaplan, Paul Cappuccio, Paula Weinstein, Pax Wasserman, Peggy Noonan, Peggy Siegal, Perri Peltz, Pete Peterson, Peter Bart, Peter

Consiglio, Peter Harvey, Peter Kunhardt, Peter Mozarsky, Peter Rienecker, Phil Schopper, Dr. Phillip Blumberg

Q—Quentin Schaffer

R—Rachel Grady, Randy Barbato, the Raymonds (Susan and Alan), Rebbie Ratner, Rebecca Camissa, Rebecca Miller, Richard Benjamin, Richard Plepler, Rick Doyle, Ricki Stern, Rob Bowman, Rob Epstein, Robert Garrison, Robert Lyon, Roberta Cohen, Rocco DiSpirito, Roger Moley, Ron Meyer, Rory Kennedy, Rosario Thornton, Roz Lichter, Ruby Hearn, Ryan Murphy, Ryan White

S—Sam Berns, Sam Pollard, Sandra and Phil Ehrenkranz, Sandy Linter, Dr. Sanjay Gupta, Sara Bernstein, Sarah McCarthy, Sarah Teale, Sari Gilman, Scott Burns, Scott McElhane, Scott Sherratt, Sebastian Junger, Shari Cookson, Sharia Walker, Sharmeen Obaid-Chinoy, Sharon Werner, Shirley Lord, Sofiya Danilovich, Sparkle Beauty Salon, Spike Lee, Stacey Reiss, Stanley Moger, Stephanie George, Stephanie Katz, Stephen M. Silverman, Stephen Sondheim, Steven Cantor, Dr. Steven Gullo, Steven Okazaki, Steven Scheffer, Sue Mengers, Sue Sattler, Susan Ennis, Susan Hadary, Susan Lacy, Susan Madigan, Susan Solomon, Sylvia Lifschitz, Sylvia Miles

T—Tammy Haddad, Ted Leonsis, Ted Murphy, Ted Olson, Teddy Kunhardt, Tess Ayers, Thalia, Thom Powers, Tia Lessin, Tim Norman, Tim Van Patten, Timothy Greenfield-Sanders, Tina Brown, Tom Fontana, Tom Woodbury, Tommy Davis, Tommy Mottola, Tony Tower, Tracy Tragos, Trish Adlesic, Trixie Flynn, Trudie Styler

V—Valerie Estess, Valerie Veatch, Vartan Gregorian, Veronica Van Pelt, Vicki Gordon, Dr. Vicki Nevins

W—Wayne Harris, Will Schwalbe

Z—Zach Enterlin